ENLISTED MEAT

ENLISTED MEAT

and other
True Military Homosexual Stories

Volume 1

Edited by Winston Leyland

Leyland Publications
San Francisco

ACKNOWLEDGMENTS
Some of the Rick Jackson stories in this volume first appeared in *Advocate Men, Drummer/Mach* and *Uncut*. William Cozad's "Cum Sailor" first appeared under a different title in *Honcho* ; Mark Fox's "Mean Marine" first appeared in *Blueboy*

ISBN 0-943595-32-0

Leyland Publications
P.O. Box 410690
San Francisco, CA 94141
Complete catalog of available books is $1.00 postpaid.

CONTENTS

INVITATION TO OUR READERS

If you've read and enjoyed this book, *Enlisted Meat*, or our earlier volumes in this series, we invite you to write about some past sexual experience that is vivid in your mind, whether from your young manhood, or from last week, e.g. my first college homosexual experience, sex encounters when a soldier/sailor, etc. But no under legal age experiences, please. All material should be based on true experiences — no fiction or fantasies. Manuscripts submitted should be typed, double spaced, from 5 to 25 pages. If your manuscript is accepted, it will be published in a future book either anonymously or with your name as byline (whichever you request). We regretfully cannot return any manuscripts, but you will receive free copies of the volume in which your work appears. Please send material to: Leyland Publications, P.O. Box 410690, San Fancisco, CA 94141.

GULF MANEUVERS

RICK JACKSON

The stories bylined "Rick Jackson" in this volume were written by a young man assigned to work in "Operation Desert Shield" off Saudi Arabia in 1991. For obvious reasons his real name can't be used, but readers should be aware that they are reading first-hand "military meat" stories.

1. Sinbad and the Sailor

WHEN MY FLIGHT FINALLY LANDED at Abu Dhabi and I stood in the terminal's dry, dusty heat waiting for the ship's van to pick me up, sex was just nearly the last thing on my mind. I knew that on board ship I'd have to keep my pecker stowed away. Some COs don't mind, on an unofficial basis, what their crew do to each other during long, lonely midwatches, but the *Dalton*'s C.O. was a homophobe who just loved to bounce faggot butt right out of the Navy. If sex aboard ship was out, I sure as fuck never thought of Abu Dhabi as a lover-monkey's playground. I'd heard the conventional wisdom that Islamic men used women for breeding and men for pleasure, but nothing about the gut-choking heat or the dozens of policemen wandering around with automatic weapons promised that Abu Dhabi was happy cruising ground. I certainly never expected that the best, most memorable fuck of my life was just minutes away.

The duty driver was taking forever. My eyes wandered around the terminal, which looked as though it were constructed in the early twenty-first century and then magically transported back to the tenth, slowing to work its way forward again, collecting dust and rotting away to bits. I was only vaguely conscious of the people around me, but I sensed them taking an interest in me. Nearly all the Arab men wore *thobes*, the loose-fitting nightgown-like affairs you've seen in Arab movies. My musings on Islamic construction and fashion were brought to a grinding halt when I saw a guy about my own age looking at me from the other side of the arrival's area. Well, I don't mean exactly he was looking at me — everybody in the room was looking off and on at the exotic,

7

super-studly foreigner in Navy whites suddenly come among them.

This guy was *looking* at me : checking out my chest measurements and letting his eyes drift down across my flat belly to size up the length of my lizard. When I saw that special look, I forgot all about the rapidly drying sweat caking my body and the tardy duty driver. My dick reminded me that although we were both fresh from a month at home, he hadn't been exercised in nearly 36 hours. I checked the kid out as much as I could considering the cotton tent he was lost inside and was almost tempted to let the monster out for a walk on the wild side. Although I'm not usually turned on by Arab types, this brown-skinned Sinbad was different. He was about 5′ 5″ with a pug nose and curly hair so thick it made your fingers ache. Something about him told me he'd have muscles up the ass — just where I wanted them. I began to wonder whether conventional wisdom mightn't have something to it after all. Those coal-black eyes reamed their way through my consciousness and into my soul as they worked their greedy way up and down my young sailor body looking for some hint that I was ready to give him what he needed. I felt the lizard swell inside my sweat-soaked shorts and took time to guide him down my leg so he wouldn't spook stray passers-by. When I looked back up, the kid was gone.

For the first few minutes, I was glad. I didn't need complications in my life. I needed the ship's van. Still, the more I thought about those full, cock-starved lips, the more I figured one last solid fuck before I reported aboard might be a good idea. Besides, I wanted to do my bit for international relations and if Arab customs demanded I prong this foxy little Arabian Beaver Cleaver up his tight ass, who was I to argue ? Since the kid had been standing near a john door, I thought he might have hopped inside to pump some crude Arabian cream.

Arab shitters are a howl. They look like pissers that are knocked over backwards and sunk flush with the floor. There's no such thing as a seat ; you put your feet into little footrests on either side of the thing, squat down, and dump. Toilet paper is often as much a mystery to them as seats. Arab johns are always equipped with hoses dudes use to rinse off their butts once they're finished with business. That's not what my little camel-jockey was using his for, though, when I peeked under the door of the middle stall and found him. Since the operation is done at floor level, the space under the doors is usually only three or four inches, but that was enough to see two sandal-shod feet, a dark brown ball-bag swinging back and forth as his cock, lurking just out of view, got the beating of its young life. The kicker was that hose — trailing down into the crapper and up again straight into that tight Arabian butt. The little asshole was getting a cold-water enema.

I was starting to worry about somebody coming in for a leak and catching me at my "Peeping Rick" routine when I heard a yelp and a huge WHOOOSSSSHHH. He stayed in his squat and that hose stayed locked inside his hole, dribbling cold water where my good news belonged. I waited a few seconds for him to start on another tankful and then tapped gently on the door. A flustered flurry of grunts and cotton rustles were followed by a faint creak as the door edged open to reveal Sinbad half standing, thobe around his waist, cock throbbing against his lean, hairless belly, and silver-coloured hose still up his boy-butt. He didn't say a word; I wouldn't have understood it if he had. The feral look of a chipmunk at rut, at once trapped and lust-possessed, haunting his young face told me everything I needed to know.

I eased my way into the stall and just managed to avoid stepping into the crapper. Once behind him, I reached forward to slam the door and jerk the hose out of his ass. My hands reached beneath his thobe as I pulled his quivering body hard against mine. My fingers slid over his soft skin and hard muscle, up across his flanks to cup his hard, tit-capped pecs. I think I heard a whimper escape his lips, but it might even have been my own. I know my blouse was off and tossed into the corner and that my pants were open to give my gear ready access to its Arabian baptism, but mainly I remember how very right he felt nestled in my arms. My fingers found his passion-pointed tits and set about giving them a serious US Navy tweaking. Shudder after shudder echoed through the hard muscle of his lean body to quake in pleasure against my own. His body was completely hairless except where it counted and once my fingers tired of their tit-torture, they seemed to glide of their own accord across his soft, sweat-slickened skin. My lips briefly explored his neck and the lobes of his ear; one hand worked its way from underneath his

9

thobe to grab great handfuls of his thick, curly hair to pull his head back against mine for some serious loving.

His cock soon crowed out for attention, so I reached down to his crotch as I had so many others before. As with all Muslim men, his meat had been trimmed. The almost Brillo-like stiffness in his pubes conjured a fleeting image of those hard hairs grinding their way into my butt as he porked the shit out of me. That waking dream would have to wait for another day though. Just then I was even more turned on by the idea of what my uncut heathen lizard could do to his water-filled oasis. His balls swung low and heavy between his legs, and his crotch was hot and sweaty. I suspected greatness and pulled my hand up to my face to take in his scent in long, slow, delicious breaths that filled every corner of my lungs with hot, musky sensuality unlike anything in my experience. The scent of the desert south of Samarkand, of caravan afternoons out of legend, of antique adventures, and sheiks in tented, forbidden, masculine love drove me deeper into a dream almost as exciting as the exotic young male body at my mercy.

My cock slithered between his firm butt's coffee-coloured mounds of manmuscle, seeking adventure more than relief. As his cheeks locked onto my foreskin like no paw ever had, every movement became a perverse and very new kind of handjob. My skin slipped up and back over my hard-throbbing head, pleasuring my trigger-ridge and teasing me with fantastical possibilities even beyond the Arabian Nights. I reached down past his Islamic meat, past his heavy-hung ballsack and gripped the kid between his thighs so I could pull him upward, impaling his yearning, straining hole on my US Navy cock.

He gasped when I broke through the rings of muscle. I expected him to ; most men make noise when Big Rick splits their butts open for the first time. What threw me was the way the cool water up his butt felt around my hot, throbbing cock. Nor was I ready for the way his fuckhole locked around my lizard so tightly that very little of his watery load oozed out. I'd fully expected to have him gush shitty water like a geyser with every stroke, but even later on, when I was carelessly pounding into him with everything I had, most of our odd lovelube stayed inside where it belonged. More than anything, his guts felt like Jell-O, yielding to my attack, but immediately engulfing me on all sides and, in the end, conquering me.

I put up a fine battle first. When I lifted him onto my cock, his feet didn't touch the floor, and I held him suspended, locked on my lizard as I fucked him up the butt while his feet dangled like those of a rag doll in a mastiff's mouth. Supported as much by my dick and my lust as by my hands, he flew along my wet fuck-pole like a monorail car bound for glory. My hips thrust him up ; my hands would pull him back hard enough against my pubes so I could hear his guts splash inside. He wasn't big, but he was muscular and got so heavy that I knew after a few minutes that he belonged on his knees. Since the only real room inside the stall was over the crapper, I set his knees onto the footrests and went back to work.

Once I had him pinned beneath me, I slid my arms under his chest and grabbed his shoulders from below. Then I gave my lizard its head. He knew what to do without my guiding every ass-wrenching fuckthrust. My hips continued to slam my cock into his tight, water-logged butthole and drive his torso away from me until, just as my trigger-ridge caught on the inside of his hole, my hands caught his shoulders and jerked him back down the length of my shaft. Every inch of his hungry hole gobbled me down like a Santa Monica pro. On most strokes, I felt my cum-slit slamming into his prostate on the way in. He would grunt that little chipmunk squeal of his and the shock-waves of my impact would ricochet up through his muscle to inflame my own randy flesh to even greater frenzy.

Thrust blurred into frantic fuckthrust ; the harder I used him, the more dreamlike the unlikely idea of me reaming out an Arab stranger in a Gulf airport crapper seemed to be. His grunts and moans echoed my own and began to rattle the walls of the stall, but my need had now grown almost as great as his. Both of us were past caring if our rutting were overheard by anyone who might wander into the john. At that point, my lizard thought he was worth risking an Arab prison — but then, my lizard always was a sappy, romantic dick.

Driven by a timeless need, I pounded harder and deeper into his young hole. By this time, as I was sinking my teeth into the back of his neck like some jungle animal, I was almost completely lost to the world. My universe just then consisted of his butt and my cock. Almost as though I were watching some outrageous fuckflick, I sensed in a detached, second-hand way how I was hunched over his back, humping away like a cur dog atop a mongrel bitch, my paws holding tight as I growled and lapped at his neck and ears. Soon even that reality faded into the mist of my savagery and I was left with a universe filled only with a burning, tactile blackness of such dizziness I feared I might be capable of anything. Suddenly, the black void exploded into brilliance as my ballbag pumped uncountable buckets of my burning seaman semen up through my cumchute and out into the waterlogged guts which stayed wrapped hard around my cock. Images from that fuckflick which filtered through the raging insensibility of my need joined together to form a flickering animation of mind-shattering satisfaction. Whether because of the very real danger of discovery, the exotic perfection of the hole I was using, the cool desperation of the kid's sloshing guts, or a combination of these and other perversions, I kept humping and grinding and spunking my load into that butt until I thought I'd fucked up a nut. My balls burned but when I started to slow at last, twin brown hands gripped my ass and pushed me back in : the kid was obviously trying to commit suicide on the end of my nine, thick, very angry inches.

Never one to let my own discomfort stand in the way of love or the cravings of my partners, I ignored the fire in my balls and pounded my still-stiff cock on for another three or four minutes until I felt my little fuck-buddy seize up like a cylinder around a broken piston. I don't know what he was howling, but I do know I felt my arms, still locked around his shoulders from below, being splattered with gobs of desert-hot jism. Something in his twisted torment drove me to the abyss again and pulled me over after him. I couldn't help adding another impossible creamy jet to his butt's burden. We rocked on together for a time, but both of us knew we were finished.

When I pulled my lizard out of his fuckpond and stood up, I wasn't surprised to see that what little of his assload had leaked out during our frolic had trashed a pair of dress white pants. I suppose I could have taken them aboard with me and sent them through the laundry, but explaining how I'd gotten shit stains just there might have been tricky. The other surprise was the sight of Sinbad's cream oozing its way down his hairless, coffee-brown chest. I couldn't help reaching over to wipe a fingerload of his jism up so he could lick his manstuff from my finger. He didn't stop there : he licked his load from my arms like a spaniel. I used the butt-hose to finish cleaning up my arms ; Sinbad rinsed his butt off before he slipped his thobe back down over his goods, but kept the water and the white swirls swimming around inside it tight up inside his hole. I quickly threw on my blouse, changed into a fresh pair of pants out of the bag I'd left just outside the stall, tossed the wasted pair into the trash, gave Sinbad a sloppy kiss of thanks, and was out the door and his life in a flash.

The duty driver had finally shown up and was looking for me. He was startled when he saw me come out of the head and said, "Jesus, guy. You're either the bravest or stupidest fuck ever created. There's no way I'd go into one of those Arab shitters. Don't you know these guys will grab you and fuck you up the butt before you can say shit ?''

On our way out, I saw my buddy leave with a bunch of other Arabs. He was carrying a white bundle under his arms. I couldn't help smiling at the idea of him wearing those pants months or years hence as he stroked his stiff brown love-shaft, conjuring in his fuck-fantasy the image of the American sailor who'd worn them while giving him the ride of his young life. Somehow, the idea that I'd crossed his path that once, certain never to see him again, and that we had shared ourselves and our understanding of what drove us both on — completely without talking of names or reasons or trading mendacious promises about the future — made that frenzied fuck in the heat of Abu Dhabi the most pure and precious of my life.

2. Son of the Shaikh

I DIDN'T GO OUT LOOKING for the best fuck of my young life. I just wanted to check out the bazaar — or *souk* as they call it in the Middle East. I'd heard stories about all the great deals on gold you could get in Bahrain, but nothing prepared me for how friendly the people are — or for Ali. Once I was out and about

13

Manama, I discovered folks here were as friendly as they were back in Georgia.

Not being used to how small everything was, I got myself lost and overshot the *souk*. I was walking back towards it on a dusty, rubble-littered street called Shaikh Hamad Avenue. It was late July and the temperature was about 115 with 80% humidity, so when I caught the Pepsi sign hanging over a hole-in-the-wall "cold store," I ambled up and bargained for a bottle with a guy that was Methuselah's grandfather. I popped the cap and sat down beside a rack of empty bottles onto a dust-covered ruin of a step. I remember racks like it in service stations when I was younger and figured it meant he'd want the empty back. I needed to take a load off anyway, so I guzzled and watched the people pass. The wind-forsaken, dusty street I was on seemed to be at the world's end. The local date was 13 Shawwal 1410, so maybe the street was the real Bahrain — despite the presence, just two blocks away, of dozens of the most beautiful glass skyscrapers money could build.

A flock of dusty brown kids fluttered over wearing those nightshirt-like *thobes* all the men here wear. Ali ambled over in their wake. He was clearly their leader and chief hero figure. At eighteen, he looked several years younger.

The kids started in with their English the way kids do when they see an American: "Hello. Where do you come from?" I wasn't in uniform, of course, but young studly American sailors do stand out in a crowd — and when you're nine shades lighter and a foot taller than anyone else around, folks tend to notice. Their English was pretty good, and they were cuter than a bug's ear, so I was willing to sit for awhile and do my bit for international relations by batting the breeze. The old guy behind the counter watching the show grinned and nodded approvingly until Ali said something to them in Arabic. The kids gave me one last friendly wave and wandered off; the geezer cackled like a La Farge watching a guillotine performance; and Ali sat down close beside me to chat.

Looking back, I can't remember anything we said, but time passed pleasantly enough and soon my bottle was empty. Once I was comfortable, the *souk* had lost a lot of its charm so I traded the empty in on two more cold ones. I don't think I'd started at that point to think of Ali as a possible buttfuck, but his Bambi-like eyes and cute smile must have made a secret home in my heart, because I don't normally buy strange urchins drinks. When I handed him the bottle, condensation dripping from its surface in the desert heat, I thought his wide, Hollywood-quality grin just meant he was thirsty. I suspect now that he probably thought I was trying to work my way up his butt, and maybe subconsciously, I was.

We chatted on some more about nothing. Soon my bottle was empty again, and I needed to find somewhere to drain the weasel. The whole fucking district looked like a post-apocalyptic ruin, but I didn't want to vex anybody by peeing in the wrong place. I stood up and told Ali I needed to be pushing on, but first needed to pee like a big dog. Did he know somewhere out of the way? He looked at me for a minute and smiled. Then he asked if I'd like to be *his special friend*. I didn't catch on even then, but figured since chances of my seeing him again were nil, if he wanted me to be a special friend, why not. He smiled again and told me to follow him. He led me around a couple of corners down a twisting alley-way and over a low wall. Suddenly, we were in a little niche carved out by the city's dusty cement buildings. The vacant lot was small and heaped with broken concrete, but something told me this was where the kids hung out. I didn't know how right I was. I had no sooner turned to face a wall and unleashed the Jackson lizard for a world-class whiz than Ali moved around to get a good and very obvious look. When I was almost finished, he asked if he could take a really good look. Since Muslim men are cut, he'd never seen a real man before and was curious. That was the story he gave me, anyway. I didn't care. Other guys have seen my dick before.

The minute his fingers touched my foreskin, though, I knew his interest wasn't even slightly clinical. The little bastard did everything but genuflect. He grasped my foreskin like some holy relic and made faint, almost subsonic noises of admiration approaching worship as he pushed and pulled on it, sliding it up and down my cock until the blood was rushing to my heads. If my brain didn't know what was going on, my hips sure as shit did. I felt them start thrusting forward, pushing my business end into his hand as my butt clenched and flexed on autopilot. Ali pulled down on my shaft, working a great gob of skin across my head to form a fleshy crown. His fingers flicked against my 'skin, driving my lust-lever into overdrive. It pulsed and twitched and bobbed and did everything but quote Chaucer as the boy's hand clenched ever-tighter around it. Ali reached down with his face and let his nose slide along just above my super-sensitive 'skin and then lost no time in tongue-fucking my cock. He kept his jack-hand tight behind my trigger ridge and slid that boyish tongue through the ruffled opening of my cocksock as though he'd been blowing sailors all his life.

My eyes instinctively slid shut in almost cat-like pleasure as I reached up to grab a handful of his black hair and shove his face harder down my shaft. He wasn't one to be rushed, though. That tongue took its time, slithering and sliding along between my 'skin and the bundle of raw nerves that my cockhead had become. I felt him worm his way into the porch of my piss-slit and then move on, sweeping down and across my head in broad swaths with his bumpy tongue until my entire universe was centered around the last two inches of my lust-struck lizard. I opened my eyes for a moment to look around to make sure no shore patrol goons had wandered through into our private garden of lust. The *Koran* talks about heaven as a green garden littered with fountains and luscious fruit. For me, heaven was in that dusty rubble-strewn lot with that boyish face wrapped around my weasel. Ali was making so many satisfied moaning noises, I was afraid someone would hear. I didn't care enough to make him stop, though. With that tongue sliding across my manmeat, licking my dick like a spaniel, I wasn't worried about much in life but getting buried even deeper inside his face.

Just when I thought my sensitive cock couldn't take one more flick of his tongue without exploding, he pried my 'skin back over my trigger-ridge, and his mouth locked around my meat. His hornet-like tongue kept stinging me sweetly, but now he'd added his throat and fantastic suck-pump to the show. When I felt his lips clawing at my red sailor pubes and my cock pounding harder and deeper against the tender muscles of his young throat, I learned how much fun international relations could be. His hands wandered back to my butt, pulling my mounds of manmuscle apart and running his fingers down my sweaty trench. When he neared my butthole, I felt my ballbag rise into his chin and knew I was about to shoot my first Arab. Suddenly, though, I felt a hand grab my balls and yank them down just as my dick popped out into the sunlight. Ali's hand wrapped around my muzzle and squeezed like a bastard. I wasn't sure what else was up, but I knew I felt as frustrated as shit on a stick.

I must have looked pissed, because he stood up without letting loose of my lizard and said, ''I let my special friends have me inside — if I can have them, too.'' I'm not especially quick when I have a load primed to fire, so to cut through the confusion and language problems that took up most of the next several minutes, let's just say I made sure I wasn't getting him wrong. Then I got him right.

He turned his back on me and leaned spread-eagled against the wall like some TV felon being frisked. My hands slid up his thighs, lifting his *thobe* up past the cutest little butt you could ever hope to see. In fact, I kept lifting just to get the whole, perfect picture until the kid was ass naked and the *thobe* was lying beside us in the dust where it belonged. I didn't fully appreciate his body until it stood before me lean and brown and ready for everything I had. I let my hands wander down across his hard back and lats to momentarily cup his cute little ass. Then they slid around to his hard, cut meat and boyish ballbag. One hand kept going up to explore his chest and palm the iron-hard tits it found there.

My cock found the way between his brown butt-cheeks on its own, but it stopped when it felt the rhythmic pulsing of his fuckhole. Ali was not only six years younger than me, he had the usual small Asian frame. I knew I'd make an impression when I ripped into him so I tried to take it slow and easy. His greedy little fuckhole, though, just wouldn't follow my lead. I tried pressing gradually harder and firmer until I'd pop through, but it kept trying to climb my cock. Finally, I just stayed put and said, ''Fuck it.'' He slid up and onto my good news like a Santa Monica pro. I felt his young, tight body stretch wide to fit me in; but he obviously needed me in a bad way.

Once I was inside the unbelievably snug warmth of his fuckhole, he kept on sliding up the pole until I was pressed against the blind end of his shit-chute and whatever was left of his hole was grinding frantically, desperately away into my pubes. He swiveled his butt around on my cock almost as though he were having a seizure. I felt his need and wriggled back, scratching the unspoken itch deep inside his guts as only hard manmeat could. A long, soft, sensual sigh slid unbidden from his depths as the pent-up longings and fantasies of a thousand and one nights oozed to the surface. I put my hands atop his on the wall and leaned into his body. My hips began, slowly at first and then with a fury born of ancient jungle instincts, to slowly slam my cock up into his guts. His butt began dry, but the juices of our mutual need lubed my way and within a dozen strokes, I was fucking away as in greased grooves.

That impossible young ass continued its teasing tango, cleaning my cock on each in-stroke by moving a muscle here or there. Each time I slammed into the end of his fuck-tunnel, I felt new, more consummate guts grip my manmeat and ripple along its length like a lyric. My hips would swing back, clenching my butt and, in the process, pushing my load just one step further to glory. My cockhead would slide up to his fuckhole again, pulling his guts behind it like a vacuum pump. Then, once my trigger ridge had lodged tight in his narrow-sized boyhole, I'd slam back down harder than ever and cut a new swath through his man-hungry butt.

When his prostate found my cock, I felt his body shiver in ecstasy. Each stroke that followed seemed to bring his buttnut smack in my line of fire. Soon the boy was wriggling and screaming in Arabic. My chest slid along his sweaty, brown back and my lips found his ear lobes. I sucked at them momentarily, but as my cock took control of its destiny, I moved down to his neck. I knew the strong muscles of his neck and shoulders could take the torment my teeth were about to unleash. I was more audience than actor now. I swung in and out on a pendulum of instinct whose arc linked his hunger with my need. His moans and my animal growls echoed off the wall inches from us, yet they sounded as remote as from another time. While my teeth clamped into his shoulder, my hands wrapped themselves around his loins to hold on tight so that when my cock headed to the abyss, I would pull him in with me. My senses dimmed and darkness fell about me as I fucked harder into his boyhole ; only the glorious, pulsing fire in my cock was real and substantial. Like some far-off star approached through the void, it grew brighter and warmer and more irresistible until suddenly my cock exploded and my dick pulled me, joyous and unresisting into chaos.

Space and time lost their meaning as I hung on, blinded by lust and numbed to every sensation except the cataclysmic explosions of my cock. I fucked and pounded and ripped into young Ali for moments or hours, shooting jet after blazing jet of jism into his tight litle manhole. Eventually I began to come back to earth and heard our screams again and felt my creamy, USN prime grade-A sailor spooge lubing his shitchute. I freed his shoulder and slid my hands across his sweat-streaked chest, at once exploring his body and my passion. By now I was trying to be as gentle as I could under the circumstances, but his hole wanted everything I had. As I eased up on the fuckthrusts to be merciful and compassionate, he just arched his back into me, insisting on a Jackson-quality buttfuck. Even after I'd drained a week's worth of jism into his guts, he wouldn't let me go. Wave after gentle wave of butt-muscle slid along my joint until I knew for sure how cows felt about milking machines. When he started to straighten up, I let him away from the wall. I'd frisked him well enough to know the only deadly weapon he had was up his butt. His hands snaked back around to my butt and pulled my lizard deep into his burrow for one last hedonic wriggle. Then, slowly, he eased his body off my cock and turned around to give me a friendly, knowing hug.

As he pulled our bodies together, I checked out his cock up close and very personal. For a kid of his years and build, it wasn't at all bad. It was only seven inches or so, but not everyone can have the thick nine plus inches of a Jackson-joint dangling between his thighs. I played with his small, boyish balls for a few moments, squeezing gently at the packed sperm-sack hanging off the end of each. I thought about giving his cock a severe tongue-lashing, but he seemed more interested in playing with my stained but still stiff stud-stick. One last thread of jism oozed out of my 'skin, and he reached down to wipe it off with a finger. Considering where my jism had just been, I wasn't sure his slurping it down was a good idea, but he knew what he wanted and went after it.

He also knew he wanted to fuck me up the butt. Normally I like to give better than I get, but since he was small enough I decided the generous thing to do would be to make the boy happy. I turned around and took my turn at the wall. I had to keep my feet far back to let him get his dick butt-level, but when I felt his hot brown thighs between mine, I knew I was in the mood for love. He made it easy on me, rubbing the remains of my own spooge on his dick before he slid inside my ass. His hands wrapped themselves under my chest and hung from my shoulders as he climbed up inside my body and made it his own. I hadn't been fucked in months and had almost forgotten how good having the right meat inside you could feel. I fixed my butthole into a death-grip and slid it along his cock in perfect counterpoint and complement to his lust. One hand held me away from the wall while I used the other to grab handfuls of his hair, pull his ass harder against me, and otherwise revel in the boyish muscles of his body. Stroke slid into stroke as he worked at my ass like an expert.

I'd heard stories that Arabs were natural butt-fuckers, but I had no idea how true they were. I know I wasn't his first, but the way he caressed my skin with his hands while he reamed my butt, the way he murmured soft things into my ear as though I were his camel on a long caravan, even the way he locked his torso against mine so every possible square inch of skin could be shared be-tween us — all this proved to me beyond doubt that Ali was a natural lover. As he picked up his ramming speed and crashed harder and deeper up into my guts, I had a sudden vision of Valentino sweeping his conquests into his tent. Back then, the camera had always faded to black, but I was sure that Valentino's shaikh couldn't have been any more natural in the saddle than young Ali. He was a great kid, but for the next few minutes, I let my fantasy run rampant. I saw myself trapped below the lust-possessed desert ruler, powerless to save my virtue from his crav-ings. I slid my hole up to meet my master and gave myself to him completely and, in the end, willingly. We came from different worlds, he and I, but a man is a man.

When I finally heard Ali's breath grow to a growl and felt the spasmodic jerks of his manmeat mangle my butt, spewing one spunky jet of spooge after another deep into my guts, my fantasy was complete. I was the shaikh's, just as he was the desert's. I reached down past my stiff dick to grab hold of his ballbag. Squeezing hard, I made sure I drained him of every drop of desert juice he had to give. I kept squeezing while he wriggled and slammed and spunked and screamed. Finally, when he was satisfied and I was full, he pulled himself out of me and gave me another hug from behind.

We held each other for many more minutes, talking in the quiet language lovers use until I got nervous and insisted he pull his *thobe* back on in case someone came along. He smiled that toothy, charming smile of his and asked, ''Don't you think everyone knows why we came back here? They've probably been watching from behind every rock.'' I should have minded, but somehow I didn't. I also didn't want the time with Ali to end so I went to a hotel nearby and booked us a room. That afternoon and into the next, we were constantly in each other's arms and up each other's butts. Each time I fucked him as we rolled together in our illicit love-nest was better than the last and, most amazing of all, I actually came to need having him up my ass as much as I needed to be up his. When I had to get back to the ship to sail off and defend freedom in its hour of need, I held him one last time and tried to explain what he'd always mean to me. Oddly, it was only when I was leaving him that I realized how much more than just a fast fuck he had become. He just held me tightly in his arms and smiled, saying that some day, *Insha'allah*, I might be back. Somehow, I doubt I'll see him in the flesh again, but I have the satisfaction that I took almost as much of him away in memory as I did stowed up my butt. Almost.

MARINE MEAT

RICK JACKSON

S AILING ON A CARRIER, you don't get to know more than a tenth of the guys aboard. Back on my first Pacific deployment in '77, I met a lot of interesting characters typical of carriers. The regular sailors attached to the ship ranged from old, overweight chiefs to wide-eyed young kids fresh from the farm and ready for anything. Pilots and other airdales were like big goofy kids who love to party and are even more willing to scrap.

The marines, though, are a special kick, and none of them was better than Lance Corporal Joshua McDonald. Josh was a big, black marine that I saw for the first time on the liberty boat on the way to the beach in American Samoa. Samoa is nice enough if you like verdant mountains and sea food, but there isn't shit to keep five thousand sailors on liberty happy. Although I wasn't especially cruising marine butt, I couldn't help seeing that Josh was far and away the choicest looking meat in the boat. He was 19 and built like an ebon Praxiteles. His t-shirt rippled muscle. I only got a glimpse of the long, thick bulge in his jeans before he put a backpack in his lap, but what I saw was enough to make me so ready for love that my teeth hurt. The guy's wide smile, eyes sparkling with wit, and easy manner didn't hurt, either. Only later did I notice what really set him apart — he was alone. Sailors and marines travel in packs; Josh was the only marine on the boat. He was alone the next time I saw him, too.

I'd registered for the weekend at the famous Rainmaker Hotel so I could drink myself happy, crawl upstairs to a regular bed, and sleep until I woke up without the aid of Klaxons, alarms, or guys prodding me in the ribs to get up for duty. I'd had some drinks in the bar and went outside to relax on the lanai and sip serious brews in the tropical breeze. That's when I saw Josh looking out to sea as he sat alone but for his beer at the far edge of the lanai. Sober, I'd have let him alone however lonely he looked. I guess I must have already been half way to shit-faced because I walked over and asked the guy if he wanted some company. Since we were the only two military types with enough class or cash to afford the Rainmaker, I figured I'd just keep him company while the brews took effect. I wasn't trying to do him. Not every marine wants sailor dick up his butt — or at least so some of them claim. When I saw his eyes start at my face and slide down to my package, the plan for the evening changed. We exchanged a couple more looks, bought a couple of beers, graduated to a couple of six-packs, and took them back to my room to keep us company.

I practically had to peel Mac's clothes off his body. The sweat-stained t-shirt he'd worn that afternoon stuck to his rippling bare, black flesh. I'd already scoped out the shape of his chest plenty down in the bar, especially after his tits started pointing in my direction. Seeing the light gleam off his hard, hairless flesh was something else. My lips and teeth couldn't hold back and zoomed in for the kill, sucking and gnawing on his big, throbbing tits. His skin was as soft and supple as the steel bands of muscle which lay below were strong. I felt his body quiver as my wet lips slid up and down his nearly purple, passion-pointed tits. My hands wrapped themselves around his chest and shoulders while my face feasted on his magnificent body. The smell of stale man-sweat drove me onward to discover the mother-lode of musk under his pits. My nose ground into his pits, feasting on the second most glorious smell in the world. His arm gripped my head, trapping my face in that wonderland of sensual satisfaction while he moaned all the while like a randy stallion at stud.

Stripping off his sweat-soaked jeans was even more of a struggle than baring his chest, both because of the way the sodden denim stuck to his thickly muscled thighs and the massive proportions of his marine member. Don't get me wrong. I'm not one of those guys who thinks just because a guy's black that he's got to be some Goliath studster. I've seen plenty of black dicks smaller than my thick nine inches. That night, though, I discovered how much meat there really is in a Big Mac — and it's 100% prime beef. He was ten or eleven thick inches long with oodles of skin hanging over the end of his stiff pecker. I wanted to slip between those ebony thighs and help the guy out in a big way, but before I could get going, he was ripping at my clothes and returning the favor. The horny jarhead sucked at my tits, lapped at my pits like a spaniel in heat, and came up for air to slide his tongue far enough down my throat to taste gizzard. When he tugged at my shorts and we were both suddenly naked, I knew the time was as ripe as it was going to get. I pushed his ass backwards onto my bed, tossed my crotch toward his face, and dived down to give his dick the justice it deserved.

His crotch was even better than his pits had been : ripe and musky and inviting. Every lungful of his man-smell was more of a turn-on than the last until blood rushed in my ears and I was within a gnat's pube of spunking off on general principles and that hard jock body. While I started high with his ballbag, he put his mouth to work on my cock, sliding his lips, tongue and, finally, his throat across the super-tender tissues of my hard dickhead. His face responded to the slightest twitch of my meat until my hips were fucking his throat on their own, ramming harder and deeper down his gullet with every slashing thrust of my buttbreeder. Much as I enjoyed the cock-sucker's talent, I was concentrating more on my own good deeds. His loadstones hung heavy and full between his musky thighs and did everything but call my name. My tongue gave them a juicy cat-bath and, before I moved on to firmer meat, I sucked each of them in turn into my mouth for the fanciest, most festive ballhandling session since the last Globetrotters' tour. I'd have been happy to suck those tightly coiled jism pods forever, but his thick black dick kept throbbing and bobbing against my chest with a come-hither message that was impossible to ignore for long.

Moving from his nuts to the root of his attraction wasn't easy. I had to pry the fucker away from his belly and, because his dick was so damned long and stiff, getting it far enough down for me to work on was a hassle — one I found well worth the effort in the end. I had to move up to my elbows to get enough elevation to slip my lips over the soft, slack, silken skin of his dickhead. My lips reaped the bumper crop of skin from his crankshaft and added that harvest to the bounty that already crowned his head in a cock-biter's cornucopia. His tender, mouth-watering 'skin dissolved into the gushers of saliva that churned around and into his huge cock-throb. My tongue found the entry to his manhood and wriggled between those black satin sheets of delight, rippling greedily between his gossamer cocksock and the hot, hard, impossibly smooth ebony below.

His dickhead was not only smoother than cut cock, but had a taste perfect enough to drive a Zen master to gluttony : sweat aged for a day, a hint of antique manmusk lurking between the tender folds of flesh, and perhaps a dew-drop of some half-remembered piss. My own spit dissolved his essence and flushed it back up into my mouth with every cock-sucking, dick-licking flick of my slut-driven tongue. Every tastebud in my head exploded at once as his scent and taste and the texture of his savory jarhead joint flushed over my tastebuds. The tip of my ravenous tongue slid by accident or inspiration into his cum-slit, already awash in sweet sticky pre-cum. When I slipped back into my mouth, strands of his slick cock-snot melded with my spit and his musk to drive me even farther round the bend. The more I tongue-lashed his lizard, the louder my marine sex-kitten sea-pussy moaned and swore and writhed and carried on like the slut he was. My tongue tap danced its way across his dickhead, prodding and lapping into the secret folds of his cock, strumming the chords of his pleasure and mine. My greedy mouth organ was insatiable now ; no single serving of his perfection was enough. His gorgeous marine meat was not a dish to be eaten á la carte. I wanted it all and pushed and prodded ever backwards until I felt the ripple of his massive 'skin slipping off my tongue. I'd peeled him back like a ragtop in a tornado and exposed every inch of his breeder to the merciless rape of my mouth. As his 'skin lay inside out along his shaft, throbbing wickedly away with his racing stallion's pulse, there was no rest for me. His hips heaved up and forced his plum-sized knob back into the tight, tender tissues of my throat. I kept the bit and his delicious dork between my teeth, breathing on the odd stroke, massaging everything I could reach with my hot throat muscles and tending to the rest with my tongue.

I slipped one hand below his ballbag into the hot, sweaty crack that hid his fuckhole from the world. The noise the jarhead jock was making had grown progressively louder and more exciting until I half expected to have the police pounding on the door — but fear of an official audience didn't keep me from pounding away on my own. When my finger finally found his foxy fuckhole, I felt Mac's rhythm go to shit and started to hum cadence. It's hard to get fancy with ten inches of thick marine bayonet stuck in your craw, but I've known enough jarheads to realize how they get off on calling cadence. I did my best under the circumstances. I felt his butthole reach down to attack my finger, felt the hips below me arch upward in one spasm after another, and, of course, had my gullet stretched wide enough to puke up a fair sized elk. His huge jarhead balls slammed into my jaw ; I felt his cum-tube swell with one passing load of creamy marine mansauce after another. I couldn't taste shit, of course ; the bastard's dick was too far down my throat for that. All I knew was that I was getting the original protein injection of creation — and wasn't able to enjoy the subtle ins and outs of its taste. I tried to pry my face off his ultimate weapon, but it took some doing. By the time I was able to stop him force-feeding me and pop his prick out into my mouth so I could enjoy the banquet, he only had six or eight healthy blasts left. They slammed off the back of my mouth to dribble down my tongue, searing his sweet-and-sour cream into my memory forever. When the gusher had petered out, I dipped down into his cum-slit, prying his dork apart for every little whip-tailed troopie that still lurked inside his heaving, jock body. I could have stayed there forever, happily hanging off the end of his dick, but I knew enough about jarhead psychology to know that wouldn't work. Once the pressure is off, marines aren't satisfied unless they have

a) orders to follow

b) hard sailor dick up their tight butts.

Sure enough, when I raised my face off his hard tower of manmeat and told him to assume the position, the bastard gave me a grin of relief. I'd seen it from troopies in every port and knew exactly what it meant : Thank God I've got someone who understands what I want — what I *need* — so I don't have to explain. He was on his knees in a flash with that beautiful black butt up in the air. I'd gotten a quick flash as he was getting out of the liberty boat, but this was my first close-up view. Jarheads almost always have classic muscles, but Josh McDonald was something chronic. His butt was twin huge mounds of man-muscle that jutted straight out from his hips and hung suspended by magic or enthralling enchantment, just waiting to offer sailor dick or tongue a home. There was none of the nasty, slack hanging down against

26

the leg shit here. Those soft-skinned handfuls were hard and firm and good enough to eat. I had to save that for another time, though. While he'd been face-fucking me, Mac had been taking care of my dick just fine. I knew for sure that if I didn't stop now and again to purposefully consider the tax code and other depressing topics, I'd have long since spooged his facehole. Now, though, the spit on my dick was drying fast. I couldn't take time to give his ass the tongue-lashing it deserved.

I slid my lizard between those hard mounds of marine meat and worked slowly down towards the center of his satisfaction. As soon as the blunt snout of my lizard came within reach of that perfect pucker, his ass warped inside out. His butthole engulfed my cock. I was inside the gates almost betfore I had knocked for entry and found myself sliding down the slick tunnel of his desire. A symphony of muscled waves rippled along my crank, pulling me deeper into his depths. I felt his prostate slide past with a bump and hung on tight as his body rippled with the after-shocks of the collision. The moans that had died away with his load had returned long before. By now he was swearing and moaning like a 50¢ fuckflick — and praying to every profane god he knew.

The ripples that carried me deeper continued until I felt my dickhead slam into the very end of his fuck-tunnel. To be on the safe side, I lay silent and still within him so his beautiful butt would have time to adjust to my naval invasion. To show me that my beachhead was secure, his butt arched up and ground his shattered jewel of a fuckhole into the pubes at the base of my dick. If he could take it, I sure as shit could. I picked up speed, letting my cock take everything it wanted. My hands slid up along his lean flanks, across his broad back and firm shoulders, and down again to possess his hairless chest and cup his tits in the palms of my hands. They ground into my flesh like flint, ready to strike a spark of passion — but that fire was now already consuming my soul with its flames. Now that my dick was thrown into forward and pushed into overdrive, I was just hold-ing on for the ride. I felt my ass clench in spasms that drove my fuck-shaft ever deeper into the marine fox hole I'd dug for my-self. When I hit bottom, a tremor rattled up through layers of hard muscle to make my flesh shudder with pleasure and accomplishment and the need to drill my shaft even deeper on the next frantic fuckstroke. I felt my ballbag swinging into his nuts with a loose thwack; the crash of my hips into his hard, sweaty ass sent a smack ricocheting off the walls in return.

I'd long since given up trying to guide my meat. I wasn't using strategy or even particularly trying to be a good lover. Just then I didn't give a shit whether he enjoyed himself or not. I was past all that. Having mounted my meat, I was going to fuck it until it was dead or I was too blistered to move. No, this wasn't about love or friendhsip. This wasn't even about having a good time. All the basest instincts of our species erupted in one all-consuming need : fuck Mac's tight jarhead butt. Whatever it took. If the cops had broken down the door I'd have kept humping away. Not the FBI or the KGB or every god in the heavens could have kept me from blowing everything I had down that delicious fuckhole. For perhaps the second time in my life, my cock was in complete charge of my destiny and, I have to admit, it felt damned good. The harder I humped his hole, the louder the bastard moaned and screamed and swore in ecstasy, and the hotter we both got. Mac's spit and ample butt juices had long since dried out ; every randy, uncontrolled stroke my friction stick made our flesh glow more brightly with the fire of our mutual need. My hips crashed into him, my dick skewered his flesh. Darkness became absolute and then exploded in a fierce, heathen fire of such feral purity and wonder that I was for an instant sure that I had snapped the tenuous leash of life and found at last the perfect world of rapture and ecstasy untroubled by any care.

Slowly, though, I began to come back to my conscious senses and felt the worse for the reawakening. Only the velvety slick feeling of Mac's flesh beneath me, the tight grip of his butt along the length of my lizard, the shrieks of pleasure tearing harmoniously from both our throats, and, most of all, the realization that Mac and I had stumbled together upon a pastoral glade where we could be ourselves as Nature intended, where we need hide nothing from the world or from each other, where any dream or flight of fancy could come true if only we'd put our four heads together.

Even when, at length, I collapsed onto the sweaty back of my muscular marine mount, I stayed in the saddle, pulling him over atop me so I could hold him in my arms and wrap my legs about him to hold him safe against the world — and the difficult future. When we'd both caught our breath and the pools of sweat had begun to dry on our naked bodies, I gave myself to him — not because I thought he expected it. Marines never do. No, for the first time in my life, I wanted someone's dick up my ass — and I wanted it to be his.

I won't say he didn't give me trouble, but I can guarantee that putting myself out for him was worth it. For the rest of that night, we fucked and drank and sucked and drank until we were so sloshed and raw and stained by every bodily juice imaginable that we moved the party into the shower. We left the room the next afternoon to lie for a time on the lanai, but the heat which burned within us was stronger than any tropic sun. We soon fled back to our bed of sin and glory to return again and again to that hidden landscape that we alone could inhabit. There we romped free, unhindered by the ties of daily life or family or duty. When our port visit to Samoa drew to a close, we went back to the ship the better for our time ashore knowing we would often revisit that sylvan glade where men could be themselves — first aboard ship and, when our paths eventually parted a couple years later, forever in the cherished glow of memory.

MARINE CORED

RICK JACKSON

I NEEDED IT BAD. When I left bootcamp, a very, very friendly DI had told me never to fuck on the ship. In the two years since, I'd managed to keep my dick dry aboard, but it was often hard — especially on this last six-month deployment. I had a man — or dozen — in every port, but sleeping and showering and just hanging out with sixty other guys in your berthing compartment can be a strain, especially when they're always stroking around on their way to and from the heads with thick slabs of sailor dick slapping into firm, meaty thighs. You see those heavy, cum-clogged balls swinging low and want to help your buddies pump their bilges. By the time we pulled back in to San Diego, even spanking the monkey every few hours didn't keep my best asset down. I headed straight for the best bar in Port Loma and found Rusty waiting patiently for an adventure to happen.

He stood 5'8" in his boots and denim with his Ricky Schroeder face and carrot-topped marine cut. The open jacket showed me enough of his body to make several major organs ache at once. His pug nose and savory blue eyes, his cocky grin with those chipmunk buck teeth, and the bulge down his right thigh all promised me a time almost good enough to make up for the last six months.

I won't bore you with the preliminaries. I had enough on the ball to know he'd want me, too. Marines love nothing more than hard squid dick up their butts — except maybe for being put in their place before they're used and abused. I'd saved up one serious mean just to take care of that. Every time for the last six months some fucking officer had shit on me, I smiled to myself and thought of how I would take my revenge on the first marine ass to cross my path. Before the bitch could begin to see six month's dust coating my apartment, his butt was strapped down over a rack that had been empty half a year too long. Ass to the ceiling, he pulled at the leather straps holding his fresh, hard body in place and growled that unless I 'pleasured him good,' he'd have my ass. I'd planned to start on his ass, but that foul mouth of his needed to be taught a few things even more. I had just the thing to show him wisdom — and shut him up at the same time : nine, hard thick inches of sailor manhood. When I stood in front of him and stripped off my shirt, his butt did an appreciative, anticipatory wriggle that promised pleasure in the offing. When I dropped trou and my lizard leaped out, I saw awe mingled with a hint of terror find a home in his eyes. I pinched Rusty's little pug nose and his face fuckhole popped open before you could say Montezuma. Before he could even think of whining, my thick dick was prying the living shit out of his tight, cocksucking jarhead throat. He tried to open up, but I just shoved deeper, twisting and reaming, using his ears as hand-holds and gagging his pansy-assed throat until he started to choke. I rammed my hips up into his face, forcing my dick down deeper than ever, feeling his hot, hunky body open to let me pass until it was racked with great heaving quakes and spasms as he tried to suck air and monster cock at the same time. I wasn't about to damage him for good — just yet.

Besides, his ass was waiting : pale, soft skin stretched over two hard mounds of marine-quality muscle. His butt needed training more than any two succulent handfuls of manhood I'd ever seen. To give him something to think about, I tore a lace out of my boondockers and, reaching low between his firm, creamy thighs, wrapped it hard around his stiff marine weapon and down around his low-slung ballbag. I hooked the ends into a loop and stuck it through a nightstick I had 'accidentally' forgotten to return the last time I pulled shore patrol duty. A dollop of spit was all the lube the handgrip needed before I shoved that thick four-inch handhold up into Rusty's quivering, yearning USMC asshole. I saw his dick and balls pulled back tight between his legs as his shitchute learned the rigid reality of his position. The long shaft of the nightstick lay hard and thick between his tender man-cheeks to remind him who was in charge. The hard plastic would also protect his tight man-hole from the shit about to roll downhill. I wanted that fuckhole stretched open, but my dick would give it all the punishment it could handle — after I'd taken care of paddling his ass good.

I started off with my hand. Belts and paddles teach a bad marine how to be good, but they lack the personal touch. There's something about having hard flesh heat my hand as I wail away on his powerless ass that pumps my 'nads every time. Not even drilling your shaft down a man's butthole bonds the two of you together like feeling the flesh of your palm ripping into his tender ass. The fleshy smacks echo off the walls to mingle with helpless grunts that slip uncontrollably from the hard body at your mercy. Your plaything is yours absolutely, to do with as you will; no terror or perversion is impossible once you have him strapped down, naked and defenseless — and he knows it. The two of you, master and victim, meld together in that moment; your souls join as one, opposite sides of the same coin as you share the pain.

I started on the sides, protecting myself from the nightstick and driving his firm muscles hard against it to smash the violence of my fury down through the hard handhold and send it reverberating along the secret passage of Rusty's tender shitchute. After the most brutal, unforgiving slap I could manage with bare flesh, I paused and let my fingers trace lightly over the livid handprint blazoned on his butt. Just barely grazing his ass, parting the fine, strawberry blond hairs that lived there, only hinting at contact, my fingertips felt like a branding iron, searing my will into his flesh. His butt shuddered and arched upward, clamping down hard on my lawman's dildo and greedy for more contact. Another brutal hand fell hard against pale, fresh flesh and turned it crimson, preparing the way for my fingers to take another stroll on the wild side. He wanted more: to have my thick dick sliding up his ass, to feel my fist clench tight around his nuts, to feel my teeth tearing at his passion-tipped tits. But this first evening back to civilization wasn't about giving him what he wanted; our story was about my getting what I needed: to see him squirm and beg before I tore the living fuck out of his tight jarhead butt.

I was sweating away within minutes. I'd worked out in the gym every day of the deployment to keep my build. Now I was glad for every pound I had pumped because mangling marine meat isn't as easy as you might think. The skin wrapped around that butt is baby-soft all right, but the hard bands of muscle underneath take a lot of punishment before they turn to jelly. Once I picked up my pace, though, his butt burnt bright as I changed hands and my cadence and the angle I used to fly at his butt. I manhandled that marine good. I remembered the knack of beating butt with glancing blows so my hand didn't blister yet his meat wrapped around that hard black rod and we started to make real progress. By the time my arms felt about to fall off and sweat was dripping down onto his naked, heaving flesh, his boyish bubble-butt had learned the meaning of misery and my attitude towards life was taking a serious turn for the better.

To give my arm a rest, I reached down and grabbed the tail end of the nightstick to jerk up and away. The relentless black handhold dug into unfamiliar territory deep inside his guts as his straight-laced ballbag and dick torqued and twisted. I left his cherry-red butt and moved back to his face. My dick slammed into his open, bitching mouth and plugged him solid. I grabbed a handful of rust-colored hair and used it like reins to hold his hunky head in place while my hips savaged him with my dick. I felt my pubes mustache his lip as the swollen knob of my crankshaft pulsed hard and mean deep down his jarhead gullet. The slut showed me where grunts got their name : the noise he made as I pronged and reamed and torqued the last six months out of my system made me even hotter. The only trouble was I couldn't hear him howl and fuck his whoreson mouth at the same time. I slammed harder and faster down his hole until my ballbag started to tighten ; then I gave the bastard some undeserved relief. "OK, you fucking jarhead. *What is it you want ?"*

The ungrateful grunt said, "You know what I want," so I slapped him hard across the face with the best nine inches of buttbuster in California.

"That's 'Sir' to you, ass-wipe."

"Fuck me, Sir." He got another rap with all I had before I demanded the magic word. *"Please* fuck me, Sir." I thought about doing the "I can't hear you" crap just to jerk his chain, but the time had come to go for the gusto.

This wasn't romance ; it was the closest thing to rape you could have without being arrested. I was behind him in a flash. In one stroke I'd pulled the plastic plug out of his pink pucker and grabbed a fistful of his hair to snap his head back hard. The shit-stained nightstick slid across his cheek and under his nose, smearing his own man-musk into his consciousness. He didn't need more foreplay; he was ready.

My thick naval weapon tore through the twitching gateway to his soul and took possession of him. He screamed out in yet another spasm of pain. This time, though, the searing flames weren't wrapped around his ass; they drove deep, lasing fiercely as the coherent fury of my ruby-red rod cut its way into his spirit. His body clamped down around my weasel like a trap, locking the fierce teeth of his slick shit-chute around my joint as I struggled, unleashing wave after wave of uncontrolled need to flood his fuckhole. Looking back, I see now that Rusty craved our wrangle even more than I did. Once the first seizure of agony had rippled across his hard marine body and died away into moaning grunts of ecstasy, he fell limp with pleasure. I heard a soft, almost prayerful and child-like voice drifting back across his perfect male body: "Oh, Jesus. Oh, yeessss. Fuucckiiiing AAAAA — aaaaaaahhhhhh." Never one to interfere with the free practice of religion, I went to work immolating his butt on the altar of my need.

My arms reached around to grab his hard, meaty tits, using them like reins as I rode his ass, twisting and bucking across the rough landscape of our frenzy. He was no clever mount — every thrust of my prodigious pride found him heaving or thrusting his butt in a new direction. Our sweaty bodies flew together like birds of prey, grappling for advantage, struggling for the kill in mid-flight. The sound of naked government flesh meating its own kind blended together with the savory, sweaty smell of animals at rut and the brutal cadence of my cock plunging deeper and harder with every stroke into hard beef. Rusty's slick, slutty guts wrapped around my swollen dickhead and dragged me down into the welcome hunger of his hole. My lips slid along the salt-slicked back of his neck slurping up the streams of sweat that poured from his contorted body before, like a jungle cat, I grabbed hold of the thick muscle of his shoulder and used him even harder. My fingers tore at his massive pecs. My legs clawed at his thighs as I answered the call of man's most ancient instinct — to crawl up inside his ass and explode my guts into his, melding our essence as we had shared our souls and pain and flesh. Our bodies heaved together, grunts and moans and shrill bestial cries splintering the space around us as we fucked on, sliding closer and closer to the abyss.

Only fragments remain to me of the next several minutes ; my brain could only handle so much. The friction of our frantic fuck was scorching my lizard to the bone, but I was past caring. I half-remember the feel of Rusty's hands on my butt, clutching at me, pulling me down against his rolling, lurching, twisting body as my thick nine inches of sailor butt-stake flamed his ass. I remember how slippery he felt as our sweat greased the skids of our fuck-frenzy. Even locked head and tail, we still slid wildly askew like children on some new E-ticket ride. I remember the shrieks Rusty made when my dick accidentally popped clear of our ass and the almost subhuman grunt and groan of satisfaction when I went home again, stretching his tight fuckhole wide. The firm, slick presence of his prostate slipping along my dick, the heat of his body trapped below me, the texture of his close-cropped hair against my cheeks as I bit harder into his shoulder — all these and a thousand more sensations warped together with the woof of my approaching rapture as my shuttle picked up speed, weaving a tapestry of ecstasy. We thundered together like titans through the sultry night, ignorant of the moment and careless of our destination. The union of our flesh and muscle bred sublime satisfaction that swelled until it pushed away all consciousness and left us senseless, slamming together on instinct alone.

Suddenly, minutes or months later, I was at ground zero. One shockwave after another washed over me. Crisped to the core, I felt every drop of my essence gush away into the white-hot void. The earth buckled and ripped beneath me as I struggled hopelessly to hold on. The heaving grew ever more violent as my guts emptied. By the time some sensation began to return, I was too drained to much give a fuck. My body was completely out of control, reaming and jetting jism and clawing at the naked marine flesh trapped below me, until I had long since juiced him spooge-less. Even then, dry-humping his tortured hole, grinding to a stop took some time. My greedy lizard had learned bad habits and deserved to be slapped around. Finally falling atop him as we both tried to suck air, I knew it would be some time before I got around to giving the lizard the slapping it deserved.

After many minutes, the night air began to dry the sweat on our naked flesh. I eased my dick out of what was left of Rusty's marine fox-hole and freed his wrists so I could flip him over. Even though his gear was still laced up tight, the hapless bastard hadn't been able to control himself. He deserved punishment in the worst way; his belly and chest were sopping with prime, grade-a USMC jarhead jism. Lying atop those massive, messy pecs, sucking at his lips and tits and neck, slurping up his creamy froth, and feeling his strong arms enfold me, I knew I was going to be plenty busy slapping hard meat around — but it wouldn't be lizard.

CUM SAILOR

WILLIAM COZAD

I T HAD BEEN YEARS since I'd had a sailor. After the fleet left San Francisco for Long Beach there just weren't many of them around. And if there *were* they were in civvies because of all the terrorists.

I was sitting in Jack-in-the-Box on Market Street, sipping coffee, when I spotted this young man wearing a baseball cap with a ship's logo on it. He was around twenty-three, short but muscular. Brown curls fringed the cap. And blue-gray eyes, brooding eyes, looked out from its beak. He was wearing a denim outfit — a jacket with a sweat shirt underneath, jeans, and what looked like hiking boots.

He stood up out of the booth and stretched. Packed meat in those denim jeans, that was the first thing I noticed. He walked past me to the trash can where he emptied his tray. Since the cap he wore had a ship stitched on it and *U.S.S. Fox, CG-33*, I launched ︰nto a conversation by asking what kind of ship he was on.

"It's a cruiser with guided missiles."

They used to name destroyers after men, cruisers after cities. But that all changed — like everything else.

"What does the ship do?"

"Protects the Connie, the *Constellation*, an aircraft carrier."

"Oh. Want another coffee?"

"No thanks."

"Have a seat if you're in no hurry."

He sat down across from me. What a good-looking fresh young man! Lonely, I figured like a lot of swabbies. Used to get the straightest and butchest numbers just by giving them a lot of attention.

"Got two hours before I get the bus," he volunteered.

"Where are you headed?"

"Los Angeles. Going to visit my brother."

"On leave?"

37

"Just finished my hitch. I'm out. No more chiefs with crows telling me what to do. Now I can tell them to suck my dick."

I always liked sailors and the way they talked.

"What's your name?"

"Frank."

Butch name, butch kid. Looked Italian. Big snozz which made me sure he had a big dick inside those denim jeans. Probably a hairy body, too, because I noticed the hair on his wrists outside the sweat shirt he wore under the denim jacket.

"What are you going to do now that you're out of the Navy?"

"Go back to the East Coast pretty soon. Work for my dad, he's got a dairy farm."

Hmm. I'd sure like to milk Frank, I inwardly decided. Bet it'd taste real sweet. Maybe I was dreaming. But my cock was definitely stirring in my crotch.

"You could always reenlist."

"No way. Fuck that shit. Man, I can sleep now. Hardly ever got any sleep aboard ship, three-tier racks in the berth. And all those fucking watches!"

"Food must have been good. You look healthy."

"The food was fucked up. Dehydrated crap. And bugjuice — the stuff we drank and used to clean the decks with, it was so strong."

"Where was your ship?"

"The fabulous *Fox* was on WesPac but we were way out past that, in the Indian Ocean. Man, when you got off ship you had to be careful those foreign countries didn't get you for doing anything wrong."

"Where else have you been?"

"Spent a lot of time in the Philippines."

I liked Frank and his easygoing manner. Clean-cut, obviously not a druggie like most street boys his age.

"How did you get aboard the *Fox* or did you have a choice?"

"Yup. Big ship or a little one. I chose a medium-sized one, a cruiser. Couldn't get me on a carrier, they're too dangerous. Could get sucked up into one of those jet engines. And the awful smell of fuel. A frigate is too small, makes you seasick and you barf all the time."

"Did you like sailing?"

"It was alright. I worked in the engine room."

"Anything exciting happen at sea?"

"I became a shellback."

He showed me a laminated card with his name on it and on the other side it said that he was indeed a shellback.

"What's that?"

"It's a tradition when you cross the equator for the first time. You'r a wog, a polliwog, and you get initiated. All day long you wear your uniform inside out and the other sailors beat your ass with firehoses and stuff and make you walk around on hands and knees and do what they say."

That interested me. I'd sure like to make Frank do what *I* said. Take out your dick would be order *numero uno*.

"Like a frat hazing?"

"Yeah. Next time you get to do it to the other wogs, beat their asses. It hurts like hell, let me tell you. Goes on all fucking day too."

I finished my coffee and looked at Frank. "Do you drink?"

"All sailors drink. But I don't do drugs. I want some kind of life. Lot of freaks in San Francisco. I had a drink at a bar earlier and some whacked-out dude came up to me and told me he was the Antichrist. Said 'praise Satan' and shit like that. Fucking weird."

"How about going for a beer?"

"Sure, sounds good."

I was dealing with a less than two hour time limit so I didn't want to waste time in a bar.

"I live just a few blocks away," I suggested. "Got some cold beer in the fridge."

"Okay. But I got to watch the time."

Just like old times, picking up a lonely sailor. If they went with you they'd play, that's what I remembered. I might not be the red hot stud I once was but I was an expert cocksucker and could give Frank-baby the benefit of my experience of sucking hundreds of dicks and making them shoot their wads.

I waltzed Frank across the street, past McDonald's and Carl Junior's, where we got some stares from other cruisers. Eat your hearts out, I thought. This is *my* big time. Reunion with a sailor. Like a cat with a fish in its chops, I was on my way.

Inside the fleabag hotel I called home, I put Frank in the chair and I plopped down on my bed with a cold brew.

"What kind of work do you do?" Frank asked, more out of politeness than interest.

"I work in a hotel," I told him, leaving out the details. The truth was that I could have been the general manager if I concentrated on my job but I couldn't. I spent every night cruising bars and the streets. And before that it was the tubs and before that it was picking up a different sailor every night, sometimes two or three. You get old fast and the time flies. But I decided long ago to enjoy my life. I didn't care about money or material things, just dick and ass — preferably big stiff juicy dicks like the one on Frank-baby.

"Do you like it?"

"It's a living."

"Were you ever married?"

"Once, to the Navy."

"Like me?"

Not exactly. I wasn't in the Navy, the Navy was in me." I handed Frank another cold bottle of Miller. I don't think he got my little joke.

"I don't understand."

"I'm gay, Frank. A cocksucker or whatever you want to call it. That's the way I am. You can run off or we can have some fun."

"I ain't never known any gay dudes before."

"You're a pretty hot-looking kid. But you already know that."

"I'm just another sailor."

"They don't all look like you, baby doll."

Frank spread his legs and showed me his crotch bulge. "All this talk about blowjobs is making me horny. You want me? You want to suck my dick?"

"I'll take anything you'll give me, Frank."

Like in a dream, I watched Frank rip open the metal buttons on his 501s. He freed his cock from the white cotton briefs. It was a huge, stiff uncut cock that drooled pre-cum.

"It gets bigger," he boasted.

"Wow!"

Frank stood up and came over to the edge of the bed. I was at eye level to his throbbing cock. And naturally I grasped it. "It's so fucking hard! Like a crowbar," I remarked.

"Go on, dude. Suck it. Suck this sailor's dick."

I circumnavigated the shiny red glans with my tongue, tasting the smegma, cheese aged at sea. Delicious! Opening my mouth, I engulfed the young sailor's flared cockhead.

"Oh yeah. Feels good. Suck it. Keep sucking it."

I deep-throated his hard dick and held it, admiring its beauty and strength while I freed his balls and fondled them. Then I licked his nuts in their hairy, wrinkled sac while I jacked his foreskin over the head of his cock.

"You got a big fucking cock. Any gay man in his right mind would flip for hard, juicy young meat like yours."

"Go on, suck it. Suck the juice out of my balls."

My own cock raged in my pants and leaked pre-cum while I ministered to the young sailor's cock. I munched on his meat, tugging on his nutsac. I swallowed every proud inch of his cock until his brown bush tickled my nostrils. As I held onto his denim-encased sinewy thighs, he fucked my face. Then he held my head and rammed that horny sailor dick down my throat hard and fast until it was a struggle for me to breathe. But I managed to hang on for the load that was coming.

"Suck it. Here it fucking cums. I'm cumming! Swallow it, cocksucker. Swallow my fucking load."

I gulped and almost choked but I didn't spill a drop of his hot delicious sailor jizz. It warmed my throat like brandy on a chilly night. It made me feel alive and powerful, like a savage who drinks animal blood.

I had to get my cock out and stroke it. I didn't care what Frank thought. He looked excited watching me pull out my prick and beat off. With the taste of his sweet cum still in my mouth, I began to fist my cock.

"Shoot it, dude. Make it cum."

My cock took the command and spurted globs of white cum all over my exposed belly.

I *thought* the party was over. We both had shot our wads. And Frank had a bus to catch soon.

"Have another beer, sailor?"

"I want something else." Frank's cock was still randy though not at full mast. But it got harder and bigger as he stroked it for me, like I'd done for him.

"You can cum on me if you want."

"I wanna cum *in* you!" That's when Frank roughly rolled me over and pulled my pants down, exposing my buns. Then he fingered my hole and poked inside my pucker.

Dropping his jeans to his ankles and pushing down his shorts, he crawled on the bed and mounted me. I looked over my shoulder at him, excited by his glazed eyes, the hair on his thighs and the big hard bone that he wanted to bury inside my hole. "Fuck me, sailor. It's been so long. I need it so bad. Shove that big cock up my ass. Stick it to me, Frank-baby."

His cock was wet with drooling pre-cum which lubricated my pucker when he pried it open with his prick and crammed it all up my shithole.

"Oh fuck. It's so big. So hard. Fuck me with that big sailor dick. Really let me have it."

Frank sawed into my asshole. I hadn't been stuffed for quite a while. And I hadn't been stuffed with seafood in ages. I wanted to give Frank the fuck of his life. So I moved my ass around and squeezed his fat dick with my ass muscles. "Fuck the shit out of me. You hot, fucking big-dicked sailor! Fuck me good so that I'll stay fucked."

Frank made me moan, sweating like a hog while he crammed my hole. He fucked slow and deep, picked up the pace, then fucked me fast and hard, causing his big hairy nuts to bang against my asscheeks.

"Oh God, It's cumming. I can feel it shooting up my ass. Gobs of hot sailor cum. Aw shit. Ohhh!"

"Take it, cocksucker. Take my fucking load. I'm gonna flood your ass!"

His cannon of a cock blasted volleys of jism deep inside me, overloading my assguts and leaking out of my fuckhole when he pulled out of me. Then I turned over on my back and without even touching my dick I shot all over the bed.

Frank straddled me and made me clean off his cock with my tongue, tasting sweet cum and tangy ass-juices. As he looked at his watch, the sailor chug-a-lugged his beer. "Gotta jam, dude."

"You're some kind of stud," I smiled, simply shaking my head.

He was out the door in a flash, his bus leaving in only a matter of minutes. I fell asleep with cum all over my body and more seeping out of my ass. But I couldn't have been happier. I'd think about sailor Frank from the *U.S.S. Fox* for a long time and I'd cum and cum.

SEMPER FIDELIS

T. BREWSTER

C ARMEL BY THE SEA, night time : unseen waves softly thudding, stiff breezes hissing through thousands of pine needles of surrounding trees. I stand where posh lawns meet a beach's sand, my cheeks enlivened by the touch of cool, moist air, my nostrils also enlivened as the surf's salt scent is inhaled — stand alone, in inebriation's glow, the tensions of a long, hard day shaken off, my spirit opening to the elements, where land and ocean meet in creation's splendorous mystery.

Standing alone, but not for long. Presently a presence is sensed. Someone has come and stood behind me. Not more than two footsteps had been heard approaching. I am sure I know who it is, and the heft of him, the warmth of him, though we haven't touched yet, is palpable, as if his heartbeat is a magnet drawing at me. At such a moment it's better to say nothing except ask, "Dewey?" The answer is "Yeah." Then we are mute again before the mesmerizing surf beat.

Dewey — in his early thirties (as I was back then), about five-eleven, still trim and firm of build — crew-cut, straw colored hair — a guy with kind of a lean cowboy's face, taut of skin, high of cheekbones — a Mid-western, usually serious face, off prairies — a face somewhat sun and dust weathered, I imagine. We work in separate offices of the company but have encountered each other from time to time in joint meetings and for the past three days and nights have been much embroiled, with others, in a Sales Manager's conference in a ritzy seminar hideaway. Dewey, an embodiment of the silent American. But he hasn't had to tell me in words that he is glad I am attracted to him. Nor have I had to hint at my attraction with words. Our glances say all which needs be said — and more than once a smile has cracked his broad mouth. But, alas, we've never had a chance to be alone together until this moment.

Dewey, hard-working, married, a father of three, which doesn't mean he is indifferent to the likes of me. Dewey, an ex-Marine, and I had learned to sense when a leatherneck desires to share

44

his sexuality with the likes of me — learned well, having bedded with fifty or sixty horny Marines in festive years, not five or so years past. I am sure Dewey wasn't one of my grooms back then, but then one was all, and all were one, and among us had been a perfect understanding — simply that I liked (like) jarheads, and they, the seasoned ones, liked (like) being lasciviously admired.

But until this moment on the beach, Dewey and I hadn't had a moment in which to test our understanding. He is about to for, remaining silent, he moves closer and, as I make no movement of withdrawal, closer yet until I feel his breath at the back of my skull. Encouraging him, I take a backward step. And then, yes, there it is, his aroused pelvis pressing against my rump. We need not say a thing. His hands glide around my waist, then clasp at my belly. I wiggle my butt against his hard-on. Surf rushes to encounter land again and again. My hands reach to touch what a male has rigid on him.

But where on earth to consummate this? We had assigned but separate sleeping quarters, each with an assigned roommate. There were thirty or so co-workers all about the place, anyone of whom might come for a walk on the beach at any moment. It had been the conference's last day and evening, and emotion packed day (more of that later) followed by a last supper, then some carousing in a neighboring bar, then nightcaps in the meeting lodge. During the convivial and boisterous con-flab, Dewey's eyes had sought out mine often. (Would this night be our only chance?) From the liquor imbibed, none of us were feeling any pain. In fact I had been on the verge of elation when leaving the noisy congregation for my stroll among the pines and had made sure Dewey saw my departure. Had I dared hope he would track me? But, for reputation's sake, he had to be careful. After all, he was one of the boys. But then, if the coast is clear, boys will be boys, and in the twinkling of an eye, at the thud of another wave, it was quite natural that his cock was freed so that I might feel of, get familiar with, what he was compelled to share with me.

But where, oh where? Surely we didn't want to thrash on the damp grass or sand. Oh, I might have merely jacked his granite hard, yet oh so fleshy, rod off, but surely we wanted more than that — instead a fuller communion, a deeper union.

Well, never let it be said ex-farmboys and ex-marines don't

have savvy. Rather than take me further from the lodge, he, with hand clasping mine, leads me back to it — that is, to one side of it onto a sheltered veranda, in a cover of darkness, though pathways on the grounds are dimly illuminated by small lampposts. Anyone's approach will be seen. Also, we can look into the lodge, where then only three fellows linger in the last of conversation. Happily drunk, the rest have dispersed, for it is well past one. Dewey impetuously lowers his trousers and drawers to half mast, and I, to confirm my lust for him, am quick to kiss the moist cockhead which has emerged from its sheath of foreskin. Hastily he lowers my lower garb and paws at my butt, then has a fingertip at my anus. Wetting that finger with spit, he begins a petting. Passion breaking in me, I begin sucking fervently. God, after four years of near celibacy, I've got a guy's cock burgeoning in my mouth, and it's Dewey's very tasty cock.

However there is still the sound of voices, and my mate is keeping watch and with a free hand at the ready to pull up trousers. Do we dare get naked in abandon and throw ourselves on the deck sofa? Then he whispers, "I don't want to come right off." He turns me around and begins moving blood-compacted cockhead up and down the seam of my buttocks, and soon it pauses at the orifice he has moistened. It's obvious how he wants this consummated. But, lord. A lubricant is needed, for this ardent stud is thickly endowed.

Before continuing with this grand scene, a little background may broaden the subject matter. I had known of my preference for the male early in my life, ever since a nineteen-year-old on our block had initiated me by having me jack him off. A year later, at age thirteen, my initiation had been furthered by another nineteen-year-old. I have never been ashamed of my homosexuality, but had the sense to know it was wiser that I not admit publicly to it in the land of homophobia (and it was still a crime in those days) — keeping silent on the subject, not out of shame, rather to avoid the social inconvenience, if not danger, in being 'found out'.

However, most of my life had (has) been lived chastely, perhaps because, like the ancient Greek pagans, I adhere to the adage 'nothing in excess'. (Except for that glorious two years when Marines out of Camp Pendleton were coming to Hollywood to get picked up and glorified, in a time of war — except then when I was blowing corn, milk, beef-fed leathernecks regularly, as well as getting buggered by some and buggering a few myself, (those who knew the male vagina is inflammable), my sexual encounters have been sporadic. I prefer a certain type of huskie and prefer for them to make the first move, just as Dewey had done. Such butch fellows are not easily come by.

Perhaps my silence on the subject made me a 'closet queen'. Certainly I had no compulsion to tell all. As a matter of fact I was sure my peers at work guessed about me, and they, like myself, held that it was best to keep silent on certain subjects. (After all, they weren't blabbing about what they did in bed with wives and/or broads.) Certain decorum is required in the work place, and I was much respected there because of my industry and abilities. And, as 'mixing business with pleasure' can mess up matters, I refrained from doing so, though some of the guys I supervised were young and sexually enticing. Why wreck otherwise good relationships. (Besides, kept secrets can be lots of fun.)

Dewey was no fool either. Obviously, on the farm and/or Corps, he had learned what two males can hotly do together and was not disgusted by it. But no married man with kids wants to be caught in the act, with disgrace, if not a sacking, the likely consequence. But here we were on that porch running the risk. Three voices persisted in the lodge. What on earth were they talking about? When would their booze and the sandman lead them off to their beds? Yet, perhaps they were as intent on mind-fucking as Dewey and I were at our pastime, the better part of his submerged finger massaging my rectum. In gratitude for what I was letting him do unto me, he let me suck awhile again. ''Take it easy though,'' he whispered huskily.

Running the risk. Were we a couple of incipient subversives?

Rebellion was in the air those days — the Free Speech Movement in Berkeley, open talk of a sexual revolution and, even at our Sales' seminar, there had been a revolt. Our company in the past two years had lost fifteen percent of its market share, competition accelerating in California's arena. The Sales conference had been called to advance the theme — 'Go out there and sell like hell.' To which two thirds of the attendees, I one of them, had rejoined, 'Hell no, we won't sell — not until we have a product to sell like hell.' This was so vehemently expressed, the consultants conducting the affair changed its agenda. "Okay, guys, we'll break up into three groups, each of which will brainstorm ideas on how a product can be created." And, after two frenzied days and nights, what emerged from those groups was a call for the top-heavy, dead in the water, bureaucratic structure of the company to be overturned, streamlined for efficiency. This amounted to a declaration of revolt against the corporation, which we believed was preventing our efforts at every turn. I had volunteered to type the manifesto the following morning in an office of our meeting place, so it could be delivered to the Home Office honchos.

No wonder I was in such a heady mood when I began that walk to the beach — headier yet when Dewey brought his elemental self to share with me in invigorating night breezes, recklessly freeing himself from social strictures. He's freely finger-fucking me now, and the bulky cock I'm salivating on, recklessly, tastes of the fecund sea. A couple of subversives, running a risk.

A door is heard shutting. Two of our peers are seen going down one of the paths on wobbly legs to the sleeping bungalows beyond. The last of voices trails off, evaporating into the sound of pine needles. Dewey inspects through a window. No one in the lodge. Only two lights burning. He waits, listening longer. Silence, except for the breezes and distant surf. But he waits a while longer, making sure there is no sound of shoes on gravel. No. Then, having pulled up his britches, as I do mine, he leads me around to the lodge's entrance, leads me into that high ceilinged cavern beneath its open beams, then locks the door behind us, draws the drapes and flicks off one of the lamps. We are enclosed. Yet we wait longer, listening. No one afoot. It's then, after removing shoes, that Dewey doffs all his clothing — and there he is, in soft light, buck naked : broad of shoulders, taut of belly, pecs, biceps and calves finely delineated through lightly auburn skin — a somewhat sheepish expression on his face, dear to behold ; and, of course, there's his *cock*, jutting up from a mass of brown, pelvic hair and above his sacked testicles his saliva glistening, peach-hued *cock*, vein gnarled and broadly domed. How glad he is to see how very enthralled I am to behold that chunky *cock*.

Might some night watchman come on his rounds? We crazily don't care. Once my clothes are off, Dewey once again has glans penis warmly pressed to my warm sphincter. No doubt what he's determined to get to. But God, without a lubricant he's likely to rupture tissue with that mass.

As written above, never let it be doubted that an ex-farmboy and jarhead can't find a solution. In the adjoining room is a kitchenette, and on the workboard are the remnants of snack making, including a jar of mayonnaise. Simple enough to apply the silken goo to fingers and begin a priming. And what a priming it is, Dewey as methodical and sure at it as the most precisely jeweled clock. A petting of the muscle, then fingertips parting the fissure slightly, then the finger moving in ever so slowly — nothing of haste in him. Then the better half of a finger is carefully revolving within, a hypnotist lulling the muscle — later two fingers in to the lower knuckles, as he considers my face gauging the extent of any pain. To let me know how very much he cares, he kisses the orifice, licks it some, then blows his breath into me. Surely the sphincter has entirely relaxed, but I have no idea how much it has opened until I feel his tongue entering. (Lordie, this guy's barnyard education must have been complete.) Then, then — the *cockhead*, a plug. Rather than force it past the portal, he lets it rest there so that my asshole will accept it before he proceeds.

The sofa isn't wide enough for the action about to ensue, so he, without words, encourages me to get onto the floor on my back, with legs up around his waist, my feet interlocked at the small of his back. He studies my face as he inches the bulk in, again gauging what pain I might be feeling. To tell the truth, he has so thoroughly mesmerized the muscles the pain is minimal. He sees he is free to proceed, carefully getting in to the hilt, his bristly crotch hair felt on my upwardly bowed nats. Not long after, I realize Dewey is ejaculating with cock held buried in place, his flanks quivering and four muffled gasps breaking across his lips, perhaps one for each spasm of cum.

Thank heavens, he's not the kind to call it quits after getting his jollies. As soon as he settles from his orgasm, he continues at the hump — slow on the draw, slower at the penetration, taking a rhythm as steady as the intermittent crash of surf in the distance. He may have attuned himself to it. How long he kept at it, I can't say, for we were beyond time. I feel as if the earth is moving within me. Perspiration has broken on our brows. Rivulets of sweat are soon slithering down his chest.

When I splatter my euphoria's pearls onto my belly, he pauses long enough to swipe them up with fingers and palm, then spread the stuff over his phallus, then more mayonnaise. I'm so well greased there is a faint slurping sound as he resumes the fuck. How much longer is of no matter, for we may have joined eternity's sweep.

There's a noise at the door, as if someone is trying it. Dewey disengages but does not bolt, instead rests at my side, listening, as do I. Some patrolling guard outside? Well, whoever it may be, there is no persistent attempt to enter. Who knows, perhaps whoever it is guesses someone within is having some fun and decides not to intrude. And fun I am having as my companion remains in repose awhile — fun taking his balls into my mouth, then licking the length of pecker shaft (never did mayonnaise taste so good, as if spread on quiche) — that cock, only an inch from my eyes, seeming bigger than the room, bigger than all outdoors. Then I am kissing and lapping upon his sweaty anus, the two of us soon avid at mutual licking.

When the hump is resumed, I think of him as a farmer doggedly ploughing his fields or a leatherneck resolute in a long march. Then I feel the earth in me is solidifying lava.

Dewey, having made a final, deep jab, is climaxing again — four short groans breaking from his chest.

Of course he's exhausted but has energy enough left and the courtesy to bring me off a second time with a hand while giving my sphincter four farewell kisses, in appreciation for the pleasure given him. After slowly dressing, moving as if spellbound, we part — with a perfect understanding that he had taken my attraction to him to honest heart and had shown his appreciation with the organ dearest to his heart. I could ask for nothing more.

After sleep, I am up at seven, hungover, and soon at a desk in the establishment's office, organizing my notes and then typing the manifesto of revolt — blissfully, since my rectum is vibrantly alive with the squish of mayonnaise and Dewey's semen — my spirit elated and in accord with the sounds of waves and wind in pines. At about ten I deliver our declaration to the waiting fellows. It is in good shape and conveys the group's intent — that is, two thirds of the group, for the other third, Dewey among them, has considered this sheer foolishness, if not corporate suicide. I am congratulated on my industry and presented with a bottle of champagne. Looking at Dewey's oh so serious face, I proceed to stand atop a table, open the bottle and pour the sparkling wine over my head. General laughter and applause. The biggest of smiles arises in the ex-Marine's eyes, on his mouth, which I had kissed in our parting.

Oh what a secret we have to cherish over the years. What had happened between us the night before was (is) much more significant than any silly rebellion. Home Office will merely set the manifesto adrift in the amorphous mess of a bureaucracy. But both Dewey and I know there was nothing amorphous about his blunt, rotund, rigid cock moving so gracefully and ardently in my bowels.

ENLISTED MEAT

RICK JACKSON

E VEN IN PORT, Fetshak and Fetterling were a pair. They
reported aboard about the same time and were both bootcamp signalmen, so it was natural for them to buddy up. They
were together so much, though, that before long the crew
stopped making jokes about how they were "very special
friends" — just in case they really were. Something about them
convinced you that they belonged together even though you
couldn't put your finger on exactly what it was. Even their division officer even juggled the duty roster so they could share
watch. By the time we had left San Diego for our six-month
deployment to the Gulf, everyone had gotten used to seeing them
move about the ship, nun-like, in a pair, sharing unspoken
thoughts and wordless smiles at the rest of the world.

I worked in another division, so I didn't have much to do with
them on a day-to-day basis — but like everyone else aboard, I
knew who they were. They stood out. One of them alone would
have made my crank inflate. Seeing them stroke about the ship
like young, studly bookends gave me dreams.

They were always talked about together — in the beginning as
"Fetshak and Fetterling." That made them sound like a Czech
law-firm so they soon became "Fetch and Fett." Both were blond
with gleaming blue eyes and a raw sexuality that could coax pre-
cum from a mummy. Fetch was about two inches taller and had
more of a chin, but Fett had freckles and a boyish surfer quality
that was hard to resist. Since they were both SMSN's (signalman
seamen) by the time the deployment rolled around, they had to
be about 20. Their pug noses and great floppy shocks of blond
hair made them seem younger, but the muscles they found in the
ship's weightroom showed they were men. I soon discovered
that neither really needed muscles to prove they were legal
tender.

On a frigate, you get used to seeing guys walking through pas-
sageways on the way to a shower dressed in a towel or less.

Younger seamen fresh out of bootcamp are used to being naked — and like to show what they have. They almost never bother with towels. The deployment was still young when I met them headed towards a shower just after taps one night. I stopped to shoot the shit for a minute so I could scope them out; I have no clue now what I said. I do remember every freckle and hair on their hard, young bodies. I'll never be able to forget the meaty, wrinkled 'skins that dangled below their dorks. Uncut dick isn't impossible to find, but finding two out of two hanging off bodies like theirs is about as likely as being hit by lightning while you're in a vat of pudding backstage at the opera. Since I was standing there staring at what was bobbing between their hairless thighs, it was obviously possible — but I knew I'd have to review the scene again and again with my hand sliding along my slick crank before I'd really believe my eyes. Fetch's dick was slightly longer. Its eye poked through the bobbing, wrinkled mass hanging low between his thighs to wink at me. But Fett's dick was thicker and completely covered by an extra-large cocksock that dangled a tassel of flesh all the way off the end of his joint. I probably only held them up for twenty seconds or so, but it was enough.

Junior officers in the Navy don't get a lot of sleep underway. What little time I did get off was spent getting off — lying in my rack with my hand stroking the eight thick inches I know best in the world, dreaming of sucking those two slabs of choice government property at once until their seamen semen gushed hot, creamy steams into my face. The images of their bodies remained so fresh in my mind that I could savor the tangy taste of their jism as it dripped in juicy fantasy down into my mouth. Sometimes I'd put those classic uncut dicks out of my mind — and dream of reaming the twin hairless bubblebutts I had seen as they walked away from me. Both sets of cheeks were full and firm and seemed to grind and squirm together like a bag of cats on the way to the river.

One night, about three weeks later, I was relieved from my bridge watch at 11:45 and decided to take a few minutes to unwind before I went down to my rack. Since Navy ships travel without outside lights, the bridge and lookout watches get used to seeing in next to no light. That night, though, there was a crescent moon that sparkled off the water and made me want to be alone to pull my shit together. Well, let's face it. My roommate was in my stateroom and I needed to find someplace quiet to jerk off for the third time that day. I left the bridge and headed up one level to the signal bridge to be alone. It's just a bare deck except for the signal shack — a little metal room about 8×6 where the SM's store their signal flags and hang out when they don't want to be found.

That's how I found Fetch and Fett : hanging out. I stood by the railing, looking out towards the water and the moon and thinking of hard young muscle as I lashed my lizard. The noise of a sump pump with a loose seal tore through the noise of the ship's engines behind me and made me turn around to investigate. There, through the open door of the signal shack, I saw two moon-struck, naked bodies folded together in the 69 position, heaving and humping away. Somehow, even a dozen feet away, I knew the perfect butt I saw bobbing up and down above a mass of blond hair belonged to Fetch. How many nights had they come up here? Even though it was wide open, they probably had found the best place to fuck on the ship — easy to get to and, best of all, abandoned after dark. I leaned against the rail and took my time enjoying the show, sliding my palm where I'd dreamed of feeling their lips. I watched as each young man's hands slid over the other's hard, lean body — spreading butts, feeling up flanks, and generally having one fine fucking time. I'd spent so much time fantasizing about those bodies that I didn't want to get too close for fear they would dissolve into the moonlight before I'd shot off. My fear eased as they grew louder. Soon their moans and dick-stifled grunts were loud enough to bore through the drone of the engines and the whoosh of the bow churning through the water. My brain told me not to spoil the picture, but my dick took charge. I ambled over for a closer look.

Fett was lying on a signal flag locker and Fetch on top. Both of them were too far gone to notice me standing in the doorway — until I slid my fingers between the cheeks of Fetch's gorgeous butt. At first, he didn't bother to count hands and discover he had a third one gliding across his flesh. When my fuckfinger found his shithole, though, his brain finally took a muster and reacted. That hard ass jumped half-way up my hand. When his dick flew out of Fett's throat, the kid knew something was up and opened his eyes. Those bright blue eyes of his widened and I heard him gag, ''It's Mr. Jackson!'' as much as he could with a mouthful of meat headed back down into his gullet.

They had seen my stiff dick outlined by the moonlight and knew what I wanted — what I was about to take. I let them suck on. I knew that later my tongue would slide up inside those skin-clad cocks until I'd stretched them raw, but I was in no hurry. We have five months before us. Just now I was more interested in the fuckfinger I'd buried up Fetch's tight, quivering butt. As his lizard lifted from the depths of Fett's throat, his butthole gobbled ever-farther up my finger. My hand felt fine sliding in and out of his tight, hairless ass — but I hadn't spent the last three weeks dreaming about a fingerfuck.

I unhanded Fetch's hole, reached out to grab his narrow hips, kicked off my trou, and put my eight thick inches between his hard mounds of manmuscle. At first, I leaned over to feel my hard, swollen tits dig through the pelt of stiff red hair that covers my chest to rub against Fetch's muscled back. I stroked my hands along his flanks and up to his shoulders. One hand eased down to molest Fett's butt even as I started to prick harder against Fetch's fuckhole. Feeling my flesh rub against theirs and their animal heat warm me in the midnight breeze that gushed through the open door, I would have almost been content to stay there forever. Almost.

My hips drove my dick harder against Fetch's quivering pucker until I had eased inside almost without knowing it. Fetch knew it plenty. When I broke into his shitchute, his body let out a squeal like a bat caught in a blender. He arched upward as the painful pleasure of my fucking dick ricocheted through his body. His back slammed me upright as he heaved himself off Fett's body to get comfortable on my dick. I heard Fett's thick manhood slam against his belly with a sloppy wet smack. So much prime enlisted manmeat lay below me that I wasn't sure what to do with my hands, but my lizard lashed deeper into Fetch's guts with every fierce, soul-shattering stroke. It knew what it wanted and took it by right of discovery. I'd found it; now I was going to fuck it. My hands were wrapped around Fetch's body, letting his tits dig into my forearms as I humped his ass. I heard Fett gag as I fucked Fetch's butt harder and faster, driving his dick deeper with every stroke into the foxy cocksucker that lay trapped below him. The thought of that meat slamming down into Fett's face just got me even more excited. I picked Fetch up and nailed him against the bulkhead, my hands on his pecs, so I could get at his butt without worrying about smurfing poor Fett.

Fetch twisted and moaned on the end of my dick like a Subic Bay whore on a payday weekend. Every smack of my hips against his hard butt forced a low animal grunt up from his guts and made him gasp harder for breath. His face was turned toward the door, though, and the moonlit grin on his face told me he was doing almost as well as I was. Fett was the odd man out. I started to suggest he hop in front of Fetch so he'd have something to ream, too; but I got selfish. Since I wanted to nail Fett as soon as I was finished with his buddy, I wanted his ass dry and tight. Besides, these enlisted sluts had probably been doing each other since the deployment started. This was my night to get some. I ordered the seaman up my ass with his tongue.

One thing you have to give sailors: they know how to follow orders. I got busy slamming everything I had down Fetch's fuck-hole and lost track of Fett for awhile. When I did notice him again, he was lapping at my shithole the way a cocker spaniel licks his dick. That tongue slid along the hairy crack of my ass, zipped around my twiching pink pucker, and slid deep into my hole. His nose ground along my ass as his hands gripped my thighs to hold on. It couldn't have been easy. My ass was pounding away like a pile-driver stuck in overdrive, jamming my joint up into Fetch's writhing body. He twisted and torqued and grunted and moaned until I regretted not having closed the signal shack door. Modesty didn't slow me up any, though, so I guess deep down I was too horny to give a shit.

The feel of his slick prostate bouncing off my dickhead, the slick ripples of his satin shitchute stroking along my crankshaft, the firm pressure of the blind end of his guts as my cum-slit scratched away at the most secret, tender itch he kept buried deep inside

his sea-pussy, the way he wriggled his butt along my length —
all these and a hundred other sensations kept my brain just short
of overload. There was the tight grip of his sphincter around the
base of my shaft. My stiff red pubes ground into his tortured
fuckhole like fresh Brillo. His sweaty back slid along my chest and
belly as his hands joined Fett's on my butt, trying to cram my
whole body up into his foxy tight ass. All the time, Fett's tongue
was dancing around and into my hole as his face smeared itself
up my ass. I fucked myself into a frenzy between the best ass I'd
had in years and a tongue hot enough to melt molybdenum.
Those incredible sensations blended together with my own snuf-
fled grunts and the slurping up my ass and the moans echoing
off the bulkhead in front of me into a warm fog that dulled my
consciousness enough to keep me reaming away long after I
should have creamed butt. For the first time in my life, I felt like
a fucking machine. I could screw butt forever.

Eventually, of course, I blew it — straight up Fetch's tight squid
butt. It was his fault, too. I'd been doing fine with his moans and
grunts, but when he started in with long, drawn-out prayers of
"YEEESSS" and "OH, JESUSSSSS," I couldn't hold back. My guts
turned to plasma and blasted out through my dick. I felt so good
that, for a minute, I thought I was having a stroke. Every nerve
in my body seemed to flame out at once until I came to, eventually, to find my hands clawing at Fetch's pecs, my teeth dug into
his neck like a tomcat's, and my balls slick with premium-quality
Annapolis spooge that had overflowed his enlisted ass to gush
back out at me with every stroke. Fett was beneath me now, lapping at my balls and his buddy's butt as my naval shaft reamed
away on autopilot. I fucked on even after my nuts were dry. That
slick spooge-filled butt was just too good to give up. I could tell
from the way Fetch was wriggling his ass on my joint like a bear
against a pine that he didn't want it to end, either.

When I finally did pull my stiff dick out into the night air, it
wasn't there long. I reached down, grabbed Fett by his surfer-
blond hair, lifted him towards the flag locker, bent him double,
and rammed my seaman-slicked joint up his ass. He let out a
howl, too, but we all knew what was good for him. His shithole
was even tighter than Fetch's had been when I started. Belatedly

it occurred to me that these two cocksuckers must not have been doing much buttwork, but that was going to change from now on out. Having just pumped the load of my life up Fetch, I was in no hurry to bust another nut up Fett's guts. The night was young, and I was going to enjoy myself. I sent Fetch forward so Fett could suck his asshole. I'd found my rhythm again and watching Fett slurp my spooge out of his buddy's butt made me even harder. I noticed again that Fetch was a twister who loved to wriggle his ass around anything you poked up inside it.

By the time I'd started to feel my next load rising, I called Fetch to sit on his buddy's shoulders so I could suck him off. Since I'd let him feel my thick commissioned dick, it only seemed fair I get to know his enlisted joint. The 'skin was pulled back slightly, but there was still enough soft wrinkled meat to make anyone happy. My tongue slithered between his 'skin and the hard, throbbing dickhead that lay buried below. I felt his need almost at once. Even before I could strip away the taste of man from below his cocksock, the slut's hips began fucking himself into my face. I picked up my own speed, ramming away into Fett's tight ass while I sucked sweet sailor dick. Fett's butt had a shorter stroke and smaller bore than Fetch's, but it was slick and full of craving. That hungry butthole gripped hold of my Annapolis-trained eight inches like a lottery check. The perfect feel of Fetch's meat fucking my face was as much a rush. Locked around Fetch's swollen dickhead, my lips sucked up a steady flow of pre-cum oozing like magical syrup across my flicking tongue and sliding up and back along his hot throb as the motion of his body swayed his dork down my throat.

Soon I was slamming back and forth like a sea-saw. Fetch would fuck my head back, driving my hips forward up into his buddy's ass. Then I'd jerk several inches out of that tight sailor butt and start the process over again. Several times, I pulled completely out of Fett's ass and let my slick dick slide awhile along the tight, bare crack between his classic cheeks. Then I'd have the fun of breaking back into his butt. My crankshaft was stretching his ass, but it was nothing compared to what my swollen dickhead could do. I knew I was going to use these two assholes often during the months again so it was time they learned what to expect.

Fetch came before I was really ready. I loved the feel of his soft 'skin sliding up and over his head, the tight feel of his man-sized meat in my mouth, the soft brush of his blond bush against my nose. When I heard his breath change from a gasp to a growl and felt his hands clutching at my head, though, I knew fighting nature wouldn't do any good. Fetch was a young animal in heat and wasn't about to do anything except pump his nut down my gullet.

That's where he started, too. I'd had his dickhead in my mouth, but he shoved it straight back, raping my throat in his ecstasy. I felt his cum-tube pulse jism, but he was too far back for me to savor the sauce. The kid "fuck"ed and "oh, shit"ted and screamed until I half expected the whole ship to hear us. When his spasms had begun to ease off, I worked my face off his dick enough to feel his creamy enlisted spooge shooting off the back of my mouth, slathering down across my tongue, and making every tastebud in my head sing harmony. I sucked the rest of his load up from his ballsack until he squirmed and pried my face off his dick. I'd long since discovered how sensitive uncut meat was once it had done its job, so I didn't take his rejection personally. Besides, I had another squid-shoot of my own cumming up.

I lifted Fett into the air and motioned for Fetch to take his place on the flag locker. Once his ass was spread, I porked Fett back down — right up his buddy's butt. Fetch had been opened up fine when I pulled out, but the excitement of shooting off had made him a tight-assed sailor again. When Fett's dick slammed through to dig for my jism, Fetch reared upward again — slamming me into Fett and Fett even deeper into Fetch. The noise and confusion of getting us all stroking along in common cadence was too much for me. I reached around to grab them both, catching Fetch around the neck and Fett at his hard belly. Then I juiced sailor ass for the second time that hour. This time around I was able to keep track of every sensation — of the way my dickhead pulsed as it launched a load of cream up Fett's ass, of the way his butthole felt grinding along my pubes, of the sounds the two boys made as I fucked one into the other. We were all drenched in sweat by now, so holding on was hard — but letting go was impossible. I shot and ground and reamed for what seemed like forever.

My prostate work must have been up to the usual Jackson standards, because Fett started to lose it next. His butthole tightened harder and harder around my crank as he juiced the butt below him. He was such a tight-ass I half expected my joint to break off at the nub. I was finishing up business when I heard Fetch say something about shitting white for a week. Later on, after we'd unplugged ourselves and disentangled our legs and arms, I explained that he was going to be shitting cream for more than one week. If these two wanted to do the nasty on board my ship, then they were going to do it the right way — with me at the helm. I was going to be on their asses until they knew all there was to know about being a seaman — and all three of us knew their introduction into the naval service would take the whole fucking deployment.

COMRADES IN ARMS

RICK JACKSON

I'M NO SLUT, but you don't spend five years on a helo carrier in Uncle Sam's navy without seeing, getting to know what cocks and asses look like. You see them all the time, and not only in berthing areas or in the shower. You see some asses that are flabby and some dicks that don't impress, but you also run into thousands that are so firm and well-formed that they make your teeth hurt. I learned when I was about twelve, though, to keep my sex life in a separate compartment from the rest of my world.

I like being a sailor. You have to put up with a lot of shit, but there's something in watching your unit in Harrier ops aboard or coming back to the ship after a visit to a foreign port and seeing the flag fluttering from the stern that stiffens the old crank. Besides, when you're a member of a group as tight as the Navy, you get to know a lot of genuinely nice guys. I like sailors as individuals, not only because they have holes I can fuck, but because they share my interests — most of them, anyway. Over the years, I've been really careful and have slowly developed a firm rule not to fuck around with anyone off the ship. In the past, I've been ashore with marines or squids from the ship and for one reason or another decided to go for the gusto. These days just the fact that you know deployed military personnel are HIV negative is a big plus. Since Uncle Sam likes to keep our bodies in prime shape, other sailors are especially hard to pass up. Even squids, for some reason, turn me on. They are usually a lot softer and usually have a little paunch, but they leave an unlearned, innate scent of sexuality in their wake which is often almost as inescapable as it is indescribable.

I've even gone so far as to have lasting relationships with shipmates, but it never worked out. Aside from the tendency toward jealousy, one has to fight temptation to fuck underway. When you're deployed for six months or so, you may not hit land for three or four of those months. If you have some hunky sex-bunny on board with you, you *know* you're going to slip away in the night to some pump room or gear locker to fuck. Most of the time you may even get away with it, but eventually the rover or the old man is going to happen by and see you with your best news up some squid's butt. Then you're both fucked. Sailors caught spoiling the merchandise can be a) put in the brig without pay for months, b) kicked out of the Navy with a dishonourable discharge, c) both of the above. Even if I didn't have condo and car payments to make, I don't need that kind of grief when I can duck into the head several times a day to choke the chicken. Now, I keep my fucking off the ship. That rule means that I spend a lot of time on the prowl for wholesome, stud holes though.

The day I drove home from the beach, I hadn't fucked anything but my hand in nearly a week. The beach I had been to is at the very base of Diamond Head as it juts out into the Pacific. I recommend it the next time you're in paradise. On one side of Diamond Head is a surfer beach. On the other side, you have a residential area. Smack at the tip, though, you have about an eighth of a mile of beach which innocents avoid. You have to do a little hiking to reach the secluded inlets formed when the lava flowed into the sea, but they are worth the hike. Some dudes like to strip for a day's illegal nude bathing. Since no one is going to stray by unless they know the beach's secret, though, the police don't care what the cognoscenti who hang out there do. It's not even that unusual for guys to make out on the beach, although usually they nip back into one of the many grottos which line the sand or climb part way up the thicket-lined trail which leads to Diamond Head Road before they get into anything really dramatic. Folks who fuck on the beach draw company. I had boku offers as I lay there with my bronzed business hanging out ; but I didn't see anything worth using a rubber on that day, so I just worked on my tan and waited. I've done a lot of waiting lately.

I originally figured I'd go down through Kahala to get onto the freeway for the trip back to my condo in Makiki, but I decided I might as well stop to pick up something to watch as I abused myself that night. As soon as I walked into the Kaimuki VideoStop, I caught his scent. The fat oaf who usually lurked behind the counter wasn't there. In his place was a dude who had SQUID practically tatooed onto his forehead — blond, about 20, 5'9", blues, very slight paunch, boy-next-door look — general all-round marine bait. I thought to myself that I must be turning into one of those lifers who sees other military types wherever he goes. What would a squid be doing working in a VideoStop 15 miles from Pearl Harbour? He must just be some kid who is the same type. They must exist outside of the nav. He looked up and said, "Hi."

"Clever fellow," I thought to myself. Then I zeroed in on the wedding band and sighed. He would have been worth a rubber. I noticed, though, that they had several new titles in and lost myself in the task of making my selection. I saw the new Dennis Quaid movie had come out on video and latched onto it. Just thinking that Dennis Quaid is in the same hemisphere I am makes me hard. I mucked about with other tapes until my clerk wandered over and started making conversation. He had seen the t-shirt I was wearing and wanted to know if I was on the ship. Was I a sailor? I admitted I was. He said he thought so; he was a sailor named Trent Christopher. We prattled on about being TDY at CCC [temporarily working at the brig] and moved from one topic to the next. He worked there part time when a buddy of his had a gig. He was a musician somewhere. I still was interested enough to envy the buddy, but my attention was still focused mainly on tapes. I noticed, though, that several other customers had come in, looked around, and left without attracting his attention. As he chatted on, I began to wonder. You've doubtless had the same uneasy feeling. If you're in a gay setting, you can tell when a dude is coming on to you and can either fuck him senseless or let him down easily. If you're in a straight setting, you can talk about how Elway just needs to find good receivers or how the market is going to take off any day now and get along just fine. The problem comes in situations like the one in which I found myself. Is he or not? Am I imagining the vibrations I was feeling? Was I fooling myself into thinking the vibrations were there because he was a squid and I have a foundness for squid meat? You don't want to move too fast because, after all, most men really aren't gay — or at least say they aren't — and you don't want to cause unnecessary trouble. On the other hand, the dude turned me on big time and seemed to me to be trying to be charming. He obviously wasn't interested in me just as a customer, else he'd have gone and helped the others who had come in and let me look through his wares. If he had been older, I'd have thought he was a vet interested in reliving a half-remembered youth in the military and was just working up to boring me with war stories. Since he was a squid already, he couldn't be heading for one of those ''what is life in the military really like?'' chats. I could think of only one other reason he'd be taking such an interest in me. I'm 24, 6'1", close-cropped red hair, cat-green eyes, freckles and am built, except for the foreskin, like a Praxiteles. What do you think he was interested in? Yet, there was the wedding band which suggested otherwise.

Since I'd finished my browsing, I cut through the bullshit and worked the talk around to fuckfilms. It was easy to do because the Honolulu DA forever has a hair up his ass about fuckflicks on video. The week before, the state supreme court had thrown out all his porno cases. I asked if he had any John Holmes tapes and he listed a few. Then I asked if he had anything by Kevin Williams or Matt Ramsey. I saw the eyes sparkle. That was it. Whatever the wedding band said, he craved me. He wanted my body. He was a young man in search of love. He wanted to party. However you say it, I knew he was mine. Yet, there was the wedding ring. I know all about bi-sexuals. In fact, I suspect most dudes who think they're straight are really bi. At least I can't see anyone turning down a tight hole in the right circumstances. I glanced down at the ring with a questioning look and he blushed.

''She just left me. We were only married about five months. She said,'' he almost whispered as he turned a red so intense it was nearly a purple, ''that I wasn't good enough in the sack.''

''And now you've decided to go back to being queer and want me to fuck you.''

''No, not . . . Well, I've never done anything with men. I've always had dreams and thought about it a lot, but I've never done anything. Besides, I don't want to get fucked. I was thinking that maybe you could just give me a blowjob.''

I think that did it even more than his looks. I look great and fuck even better. Here was this squid who was pulling a ''I don't do anything but I want you to eat my wad'' shit on *me*! You have to figure a dude with balls like that has to have a dick to match. I started laughing and asked him if he knew where my beach was. I have a rule against letting dudes I'm not sure of know where I live. After I'd described how to get to the beach, he said he could find it. I told him to meet me there at 9 that night and we would see what happened but that I wasn't promising anything. Meanwhile, Dennis Quaid, my hand, and I had an appointment at home.

I got to the isolated beach at about 8:55 and was pleased to find the tide was out and a three-quarters moon was up. Nature was cooperating. I'd brought a couple of blankets, two six-packs of beer, and a tube of KY-Jelly, enough to make me set for the night. The kid was early, sitting on a rock, looking around as though he were late for his execution. I got his attention and yelled for him to come over to a nook which is sheltered from the wind. I stretched the blankets out, tossed him a Foster's, and told him to strip. He didn't like the sound of that much and was obviously feeling awkward at showing dick, but since I was getting naked, too, he went along. I lay down and pulled him to me, wrapping an arm around his shoulder and throwing a leg over his to share his warmth. He seemed uncomfortable having me so close; perhaps there really was some truth to his "but I've never done anything like that before" spiel. My original plan was to fuck the shit out of him and then, when I was finished with his ass, maybe do it again. Seeing him lying shivering slightly in my arms, though, the same mating instinct which kept our hominid ancestors secure in their insecure world took over. Have you ever noticed that you can fuck eighty-seven guys in a row and not care whether they go up in flames when you've done with them, but if you lie quietly and hold him in your arms, looking down into his face and using the language of lovers, your protective instinct is thrown into gear? Well, if you haven't, I have; and that was keeping me from nailing him and moving on.

I don't remember all of what we murmured. I know he was going on at length about his wife. His cock just wouldn't stay up inside her unless he thought about all the hard, sleek bodies he saw every day aboard ship. As he was pumping away into her, he was too distracted to do the little things that made someone a good lover. She was afraid he didn't love her, that he didn't think she was pretty or desirable, or — worse — that he was already fucking around with someone else. There was no way he could tell her the real problem and so they drifted apart. As we worked our way through the Foster's, we talked of the nav and of the Corps and of the places we had been. We spoke of many other things that night as we learned each other's innermost thoughts, but many of Trent's confessions have no real bearing on my story and my confessions are none of your business.

Let's just say I told Trent about some of my sexual history. Before I had gotten very far, his cock was up and ready for action. By this time, I knew that he had won me over. I felt he had spoken the truth about his past and wasn't about to take advantage of his pain to get another hole to fuck. If I was his first man, I would make sure he remembered me with thanks and affection for a long time.

I let my hand cover his seven or eight thick inches and held him as our conversation wound down. As the moon looked down on us, blinking off the water at our bodies intertwined on the beach, I positioned myself between his smooth, muscular legs to take him into my mouth. A lesser man could not have done the job. His head was good. As I flicked my tongue around it and prodded him in its eye, he lay his head back onto the blanket, closed his eyes, and began to make odd animal noises. My lips, mouth, and throat took him in their turn, and soon his hips were rocking upward to force himself deeper and deeper down my gullet. One hand wandered north to flit across his hairless belly and chest to find his hard, throbbing tits. I don't think he had ever noticed them before; at least he seemed taken aback when I started tweaking them. The surprise turned to a wide smile, though, as I attacked his body on several fronts. The southern front began with his heavy balls. I don't think he had cum in weeks. He had mentioned in passing that he was ashamed to beat off (which shows you something about his level of sophistication right there). I thought that meant that he beat off and felt guilty; it never occurred to me that the dude wouldn't throttle his own weasel when he felt like it. If that's the state things have come to, then world has fallen on hard times.

As his thrusting began, the southern front advanced between his flanks to explore his crack. All right, so I'd decided not to fuck the dude; I didn't say anything about fucking with him. I deserved some pleasure, after all. As his cock slid down my throat, his hips tilted and his ass flew into view. I was able to

66

work my fuckfinger far enough down his crack to find the pucker. I had barely begun massaging his hole when I felt his rhythm change and knew that the end was near. I grabbed a tit and squeezed, put my fuckfinger against his hole, and got ready for the flood.

I nearly fucking drowned. I've seen loads before, but this dude had the highest flood level this side of Johnstown. I heard him ''FUCK''ing and using the name of every deity he knew in what I took to be prayers of thanks. Once he began to shoot, each time my face crashed into his golden pubes, the skin of his cock streched tight and his head blasted buckets down my throat. There was no way I could even get a taste — he spurted directly down my throat. When I felt his first protein injection, I shoved my fuckfinger into his ass up to the middle knuckle and curled it around inside him. Each time he pronged into my throat, I pulled outward with my finger and twisted his sphincter as I was twisting his tit with the other hand. He went wild, thrashing around and ''SHIT''ing or ''FUCK''ing like a four-dollar whore on acid. His seizures grew so frantic that he jerked his head out of my throat and began spunking directly into my mouth. I didn't mind this development at all. It had been months since I'd let anyone cream my mouth, so I was overdue. He was so sweet that at first I thought he had the clap. Even if he had, the load was worth a few shots. As it turned out, though, he was just a sweet little squid.

After he had thrashed about for what seemed like ages, he finally ran dry. I moved up to hold him in my arms again by way of reward. As he lay his head on my chest, we shared another beer as he recovered. I asked him if he thought the blow job was worth the trouble and he babbled on about how great it was, how great I was, and how great the world was now that he had found me. I'd heard the same thing forty-seven dozen times before, but he made the words seem new. His one concern was that his crank was still up ; he was so used to having to work at keeping it up, the idea that he could come and still have a hard on blew him away nearly as much as I had done. I told him I often stayed hard through three or four bouts with Cupid. I was just barely listening when I heard myself ask him if he wanted to fuck me. I'm not sure why I asked. I don't really like to be fucked ; I've never gotten off on the pain. Some dudes are bottoms and some are tops. In a pinch, I'll agree to a fuck by way of trade off if I really crave some dude's ass, but this was the first time I've offered myself. I'm a top. Since I expected I'd have to use my hand and Dennis Quaid after I got home, I chalked my offer up to a lapse in judgement caused by the Foster's.

Upon reflection, though, maybe more really lurked behind my willingness. I think I liked being his guide along a strange road. He had some boy-next-door quality that made me care what happened to him, want to please him, and want him to get what he needed. He was like the little brother I never had. For the first time in my life, I'd enjoyed giving someone else pleasure almost as much as getting off myself. Looking back on the night now, I think I had begun falling in love with him. I knew I lusted after his body, but I'd lusted after many men. His honesty and innocence and vulnerability were the ties which bound me to him and which made me offer myself, hoping in spite of myself that he would use me to find pleasure and, in turn, make me a more complete person. It wasn't just his dick or his cum I needed, I neeeded his simplicity, his trust, and his affection. He mattered to me.

He was all for the idea of fucking me. I explained he would have to go slow as he moved between my legs and put his cock against my hole. I'd lubed him good, but he hurt like a bastard going in. He grinned like a boot camp in a Subic massage parlour as he tore into me. I kept yelling for him to slow down and finally had to dig my heels into his butt to hold him against my ass. Despite what his wife had said, he had damned good technique. He would pull the monster nearly out of my ass and then crash down all the way, pinging my prostate on the way. Just as I knew he was going to rip through the end of my shit-chute, I'd feel his pubes tearing like a Brillo pad into what was left of my hole as he ground his cock around in my guts. After every grind, he would slip nearly out again and repeat the process, slapping his ballbag against my ass with a SMACK that echoed off the lava walls of our nook. I reached up for his tits again and felt him quicken in appreciation. Knowing that I would hurry him up, I pulled his head down to rape his mouth with my tongue. At first I think that freaked him out, too, but he was a quick study. I moved up to his ear and used my modified world-champion Venus Butterfly technique in his ear canal.

I've had marines nearly pass out from having their ears raped by my tongue. Trent started "SHIT"ing and "FUCK"ing again and, just as my ass was about to ignite from pole friction like a boy scout's tenderfoot fire, I felt his load salve my hole. He blasted against the walls of my guts on every down-stroke and enough richocheted off my shit-chute walls to stick to his cock on the up-stroke that my friction-fried ass felt much better. The pain, though, had long since turned to pleasure and, despite myself, I felt my cock harden and my balls contract. I was like a bull being milked for stud — his cock raped my ass and made me cum without touching my cock. I shot off onto my belly and spurted up onto both our chests and onto our faces locked together. He pumped and ground and moaned and "FUCK"ed for what seemed like hours until he gave up and pulled his cock, still firm, out of the ruins. We were a mess.

He said that if his wife had known how to do the ear business, he'd have been harder than a paymaster's heart. I took the compliment and pulled him back into my arms so I could perform some more lingual-aural gymnastics. As we thrashed together, rubbing our stained cocks against each other's even more stained bellies, he suddenly stopped, reached around to cup his hands around my ass and said, "I want you to fuck me." I told him he didn't. I explained the pain; he said he wanted me inside him. After all my noble resolve, he wanted to be reamed. Go figure life.

I obliged. I rimmed him for a few minutes, introducing him to another new sensation and getting myself even harder in response to his wild, musky taste. He's such a quick study that he'd become the best rimmer I've ever felt, so my bread cast upon the waters came back with a tidal wave of French loaves. After he was thoroughly moistened, I slathered lube over my asset and went to serious work. I fucked him hard and fast and deep. His ass must have been virgin. It was super-tight. If he hadn't been so turned on, he would probably have gone into shock from the pain. As it was, his brain misread the pain as pleasure and he went wild again. As I pounded into him, he jerked himself off and we managed to cum at more or less the same time.

We collapsed together into each other's arms for the last time that night on the beach. We talked for a few moments and then both slipped unknowingly and against our wills into a deep sleep. We awoke woven together under a blanket just after dawn when a man walking his dog down the beach had some unflattering things to say about "Goddamned fucking queers." I took Trent back to my place for breakfast. We had waffles, coffee, and cream. He moved in later that week. He bought me a wedding band to match his. I think that may be going a tad far, but I wear the thing. It makes him happy and, besides, I like to look at it and think of him when he's not around. Trent has taught me how to love ; I've taught him a few things, too. Most of all, we've been teaching each other how to be true comrades in arms.

ON LEAVE

MARK FOX

"**Y**OU GOT SUCH A HARD, hairy butt, Mark," Russell told me, his kisses breathy and light against my asscheeks. "Just like I remember it. Round and sweet. Lift it a little for your old pal. Yeah, like that. Hairy crack all wet with sweat. Sweet as candy."

Pressing my face into the floor, I lifted as Russ split my cheeks, his mouth brushing against my ass until his tongue dabbed into the crack. He worked slowly, gently, his tongue lapping down to barely stroke the skin, then deeper, tasting the sweat and drinking it down, smoothing his way lower until he nicked my hole and I raised higher. His spit washed down over my balls and he did it again, more eagerly each time, until he was stabbing up inside the ring and wriggling, working me out as I humped against his face.

Pulling up, Russ ran his fingers along the tender, slickened crack, tickling me. A finger was teasing it, the tip flicked in then out, my hole clenching and relaxing more each time. Pulling my knees up, I raised my ass higher, setting my legs, my swollen, drooling cock dangling between my thighs.

"I've missed it, Russ," I told him. "Miss what you do to me a lot. You gonna give me a taste of that fat cock of yours before you start ramming? You know, I've missed that just as much."

Russell laughed and slapped my butt hard, shuffling toward my head on his knees. Without changing position, I raised my head, his black cock waving in the air, jutting from his flat gut. The crimson head was wet and slick, the shaft a darker black than his body, his pubes a knotted mesh of hairs.

Reaching out, I wrapped my hands around his thick, rubbery ballsac, pulling him forward so his husky body soared over mine. Opening wide, I wrapped my lips over the head and wet it down, drinking in the bitter, woody taste as he fell forward, curving over my head and shoulders.

I licked down the hard shaft, wetting the sticky, twitching skin. Raising my head, I opened my mouth and swallowed the head, pressing down until the tip bumped my throat and my nose was filled with the coarse, musky hairs. Russ groaned, his balls jumping in my grip, a pungent taste rising in the back of my throat as his massive body shivered and he pulled back.

Holding my head still, I let his cock fuck forward between my lips, the slick black cock riding into me in long, drawn swings, easing in and out as he teased himself up harder. Two fingers were working my asshole with grease, jabbing and wriggling even with his thrusts into my face.

"Oh, you do me so right, Mark. Gotta get into your fine ass, gotta get into that tight hole of yours. You know I'm gonna do you right. Gonna make you feel like there's nothin' better."

Pulling his cock free from my lips, Russ stood up and greased his cock up as he walked back between my raised ass. I stood up and propped myself between the windows. We were in the front room of my house, upstairs. It was the room Russell liked the best because it was still in its original unrenovated shape. Dropping my forehead against the peeling plaster walls, I waited, relaxing my body as he stroked the back of my thighs and nudged my hole with the fat head of his meat.

Letting out my breath, I pressed back against his cock, impaling myself as the thickness spread a warmth up into my guts. Shifting, Russ fell forward and sunk into me, gouging out my ass until his bush was scraping my crack.

Deep in my bowels, his cock filled me like heat pumped through my thighs and up my back. Russ let out a roar and fell solid onto my back, his arms clenching around my chest and grabbing at my nipples as he kissed my shoulders and held still.

Russ fucked me slowly, his long, thick cock rolling out and then pumping back inside, lingering over his thrusts, drawing out his movements as he cooed and sighed in my ear. His dick probed my guts, pressing out streams of spunk that dripped down on the bare, dirty floor. Reaching under me, he wrapped his hand over my meat and smoothed the come back over its length, working my hard even with his rhythm.

Lifting off my back, he positioned his hips and sped up slowly, his cock jabbing then punching into my body, rocking and battering me until I was numbed and could do nothing but moan and drop back against him. Working my cock hard, he was drawing me close, wrenching out the come that boiled up inside me. I stood up and he snapped an arm around my chest, curving me into his chest, my head dropping back and licking his face as the taut muscles flexed against my shoulders.

His hips were flashing now, slamming into my butt and plugging me, flooding my body with a hollow tingling that shot like sparks of light through every nerve. His hand was ripping over my cock until the skin burned, then slipping down to tug and stroke my balls.

"Shoot off for me, shoot that fat fuckin' cock of yours 'cross this floor. Come on, Mark, I wanna see that spunk pour outta this fuckin' muscle man bastard. Got my fat cock rammin' up your tight, round butt, fuckin' up inside this man, makin' you feel so good, makin' your guts jelly with this black dick. Feels so good, makin' me wanna fuck this butt forever, shove my whole body up this tight fuckin' hole. Gotta juice ya, Mitch. Gotta juice your ass. Lemme see ya shoot off on this man's fuckin'.''

His fist was a dark blur as it stroked the come out of me, my body tensing and rolling back against his as he bit into my shoulder and watched. With a howl, I felt that blue light cut through my balls and the explosion rumble up my shaft. My come spurt out in a long, creaming white streak that splashed over the wall and floor, the waves bashing over me, my cock jerking and twitching as the spunk blew out, spewing down in thick white gobs, dribbling back and wetting Russell's fist as he wiped it back on my slowly softening cock, his own dick still thrusting up into my clenching ass.

Gripping me around the hips, Russ grunted and then roared, his cock stuffed up rock hard and stabbing my guts as his spunk poured thick and rich from him, his hips jabbing sharply with every spasm. His hands were gripping my chest, squeezing the muscles and pulling hair as he unloaded into the rubber stuffed up my ass, his cock moving against my raw nerves, sleek and slippery with sweat and lube, rocking as it slowly softened, popping it from my clench with a shiver and pulling me down to lay beside him, breathless.

Most of the time I was alone working on renovating my house.

Russell only came through town once in a while, staying a couple days then gone. But whenever he came by, we fucked like rabbits in the front room because it gave him that extra bit of ambiance. Two days later, though, he was gone and I was spending the Saturday recuperating.

I was upstairs when the doorbell rang. It was one of those late summer afternoons where the sun came on strong but the breeze took the steam out of it. I was in the front room in nothing but running shorts reading.

I didn't worry about opening the front door even though my neighborhood wasn't the most elite. I had lived there almost four years, renovating my small house while others around me did the same. The crime had moved out and though not a wealthy neighborhood, the streets were clean.

"Hey! Mark!"

It was Manny Logan. I hadn't seen him in a couple years, having just moved away when I bought my house and started renovations. Standing in my doorway, he looked the same, his dark, handsome face edged now with a beard, his thick, crinkled hair cut short and wavy along the top and sides and left dangling in a thick, curling tail against the back of his neck.

"Come on in," I told him, opening the screen door and taking his hand. His grip was strong, his bulky body wrapped in baggy cotton shirt and pants. Last time I saw him, he was big and on the pudgy side and his clothes did nothing more than make him look chunkier.

"I thought you were in the army," I said when he came in.

"Still am," he told me with a shrug. "Got two week's leave."

"Yeah?"

"Insubordination." Then he winked at me. "Now I'm home."

Manny was part Spanish, part Indian, part Greek, all the features coming together and leaving him with a strong build and face, hazel eyes and dark, thick hair. He had helped me my first summer working on the house. I never made an issue out of being gay around him, even though given the chance, I would have made it with him. But he was seen around with a couple girls and his head was aimed for the army, so I didn't try anything. I don't like trade; if he wants it, he's gotta go fifty-fifty.

"So what are you doing now?" I asked as we sat down.

"Not a whole lot. You still working on the house?"

"Yeah. I'll show you around."

Handing him a beer, I showed him the work I had done on my own and what else needed to be done. I had finished the downstairs and one room on the second floor, ripping out the old plaster and putting up new drywall.

"Nice work," he said, nodding and patting the unpainted walls. "Almost as good as mine."

"If you're looking to make extra money while you're on leave, I could use a hand."

"Sure," he said, moving into the unfinished room. There was a bow front window just big enough for a small desk and fit with windows on all three sides. "Hey, you can see my place from here."

He was right. If you stood in the front window, you could see over to his place and even into the second floor window. I never thought about anyone looking in — tattered curtains still hung in the window. But the way he said it made me cautious.

He stood in the window a while longer looking down into the street, then finished his beer and tossed it into the pile of rubbish on the floor.

"When you want to start?" he asked.

"How about now?" I asked.

With a shrug, he nodded and shook my hand. We started by tearing into the old walls and carrying the rubbish to a dumpster I kept at the end of my property. It was stuffy with the flying plaster and we were both caked with sweat and dirt by the afternoon but managed to clear most all the old work out of the way.

We had our beers and talked a little longer about what else needed to be done and then Manny went back across the street to his place. I was sweeping up in the front room when I saw him come in his room across the street, his dark skin pale with plaster dust.

I stood back a little from the window and watched as he stripped his shirt off. The army had done one thing for him — taken the chunks out of his body and smoothed him out. His chest was solid as stone, the pecs rounded and heavy and his stomach flat and ribbed, a few thin strokes of black hair crossing along the ledge of his chest and roping down from across his stomach and into his fatigues.

He didn't look up toward me but stooped to remove his heavy combat boots, standing again and unsnapping his pants, peeling them down his thick legs and kicking them away. His legs were heavy and muscled like his chest, his ass through the loose, yellowing jockeys firm, denting on the side as he pulled his pants off. He ran his hands over his Army crewcut and grabbed a fresh pair of jeans and a shirt, trudging out the door and into the far bathroom out of sight, his huge, powerful body rocking as he walked.

I didn't say anything about it the next day when he came over and we cleaned and prepped the joints for the new drywall. I watched him closer now knowing what he was like under the fatigues. He caught me looking at him a couple times and grinned, his handsome, broad, brown face lighting up.

"They didn't let you keep that long hair in the army?" I asked him.

He reached back and touched it. "Nah. Cut it off. It's just grown back."

"Looks good."

He smiled shyly and licked his lips a little. "Hell, can't look that good with all this dirt on me."

I shrugged and left it alone.

"You gonna use this room as your bedroom?" he asked.

"Maybe."

"You know, I can see it from my room, too. Like you can see mine."

I wasn't sure what he was hinting at and couldn't read much in his hazel eyes but he was smiling under his beard.

"Think this would make a good bedroom?" I asked him. "Might be a little small."

"Your ass ain't that big," he laughed. "It's got plenty of room to fuck around in."

"You think so, huh," I said, crossing my arms and looking at him.

He stood up, brushing the dirt from his chest and thighs, his eyes square on mine. "Bet I could prove it, too."

Manny hooked his thumbs into his front pockets and let his fingers dangle against the soft mound in the front of his jeans. He tossed his head back and was looking down at me through his half closed lids.

We were both sweaty, covered with dirt and dust, the air stagnant even with the windows open and the fan running. I stayed where I was without moving. If he wanted to prove it, he was going to have to make the first move. I wasn't as strong as he was but I could see myself equally matched to him.

Slowly, Manny turned his head down and brought his hands away from his crotch, fitting them back into his rear pockets and wandering closer idly. I stayed where I was and he crossed until his shoulder bumped mine and we were standing almost side by side facing opposite ways.

I could smell the musky sweat on him and feel the warmth of his body. Turning his head slightly, he brushed my ear with his lips and took the lobe between his teeth. I uncrossed my arms and rested a hand on his hip as his thumb hooked the top of my pants and his fingers lightly skimmed my fly.

"Ya gonna give me a fuck? Seen ya get it from that pal of yours. Know you go for a big cock up your ass. Gonna give me a piece of that pretty butt of yours?"

"You gonna go down on it, Manny?" I asked him. "Don't get fucked unless I get sucked first."

Manny laughed lightly against my face. "That ain't my bag. Ain't sucked no man. Did some foolin' when I was a kid. But I never sucked nobody. That's the truth. Couple guys in camp did me when they thought I was sleepin', but I didn't do none of them back."

"You know you gotta do me," I told him solidly.

"Ya gonna give me a piece of that ass?" he moaned again, turning and rubbing his thickening cock against my hip. "Seen ya get it. Looks so nice and sweet." His hands were stroking over my ass slowly as he whispered and moaned. "But I ain't done a man's. Ain't what I'm into."

I moved away from him and leaned back against the wall. He crossed his arms again and watched me, setting his legs apart and waiting. I pulled my shirt away and kicked my shoes off. His eyes watched closely as I unbuttoned my jeans and peeled them away, standing naked in the room. Reaching down, I scratched under my balls, my cock half hard and my balls tightening.

Manny started undressing as well, staring me hard in the eyes as his thick, blunt fingers worked his shirt, boots, and pants off, standing only in his loose, stained jockeys, the outline of his thick cock showing against the seam. He bunched and flexed his broad, rounded muscles, the sweat making them shine, then moved closer to me so I could smell the warmth rising from his dark, near naked body.

I reached out and cupped his cock in my hand, the heat wet against my palm, the veins filling and moving as I squeezed. Manny shuffled closer and his chest touched up against mine as I worked the cotton against his meat, stroking him as he hardened. His forehead was resting against mine and I bent my head up, my lips pressing his.

He wouldn't open his mouth as I kissed him, my fingers working against his cock as my other hand slid under the seam against his thigh and back against his hard ass, the crisp hairs rasping as I squeezed the cheek. Manny let out a steaming gush of air and opened his mouth against mine, shoving me back against the wall and wrapping my lips in his. His hips ground up, pinning my hand between our cocks, and his tongue stabbed into my mouth, filling it and stroking inside my cheeks and along my gums.

Wrapping both hands around my ass, he dry humped against me, his massive chest sticky against mine, the skin sliding together, the muscles twitching and rolling. Pressed together, he was twice the size of me, his body firm and rounded under my hands, the glowing brown skin satiny as a weathered rock.

Reaching between our grinding bodies, Manny's hands gripped my cock, holding it tightly and tugging, the other sliding up against my balls and stroking them. He was kissing me with light, easy strokes, his tongue brushing my lips, his mustache and beard rasping and wet as he licked down along my jaw and back into the hollow of my throat.

"Let's go into your room." he whispered hoarsely in my ear. "Don't want people seein' this."

Following the burly curve of his back, I walked behind him down the short hall to my bedroom. The blinds were still pulled and the bed unmade. Coming in, Manny turned and held my shoulder strong enough to bruise it.

"Nobody can see us in here, right?" he asked.

"Yeah," I told him.

"O.K.," he said with a sigh. His fingers drifted down over my chest, the tips tickling as they edged out the underside of my pec. "Ya gotta nice body, Mark. Strong bastard. Feels good. I . . . I ain't done this since I was a kid. But been meanin' to. I'm gonna trust ya. Sometimes, I think about doin' it. And then I saw ya with that guy and I got so horny I shot off twice watchin'. Figured I wouldn't mind tryin' it if I got to trustin' ya."

"I'm not just gonna let you fuck me." I warned him. "You're not just gonna fuck me and that's it. You gotta work me back."

He smiled a little. "Yeah. I know."

His darkly tanned fingers wrapped around my shaft and lightly stroked it, letting the skin roll in his hand, squeezing out the tip and rubbing his thumb on the wet drop that came out. With a light push, he laid me back on the bed and then sat down beside, his hands jacking me hard.

Taking a breath, he pressed his head down against the base of my shaft like he was diving underwater, his tongue lapping out and wetting my shaft, his lips slipping closed as he worked his way up my hard. I could feel the tickle of his spit sliding down against the sides of my balls as he wetly kissed his way along my cock.

Pulling himself full on the bed, Manny lapped up my cock with long strokes that started with my balls and glided the full length until his lips were pursed around the head and his teeth chewed a little. Opening wide, he tried stuffing down my cock deep into his throat and gagged, his teeth ripping against the sides.

I took his head in my hands and eased him back up, letting him take it bite by bite, telling him to hold his cheeks in and suck back a little as he swallowed. His short hair was soft in my hands, the ponytail thick and silky as I rolled my fingers through it. As his throat opened, Manny began to bob down, gulping and squeezing until his lips were clamped onto the base and his nose was buried in my bush.

His hands were sliding along the backs of my thighs, wiping the spit in as it dripped down. Taking my cheeks in his palms, he squeezed and massaged them, his fingers flitting over the crack and his thumb dabbing against my hole.

I was getting too close, the warm suction on my cock drawing my come out, his fingers working into my asshole and setting me off. Holding his head firmly, I lifted him off my meat, his spit-soaked beard dripping as he kissed my stomach and began sucking and nibbling my nipples.

Rolling against his beefy chest, I got him on his back, his legs spreading and his hands still wrapping my ass. Pushing my legs down, I lay flat over him, our naked bodies warm and slick, his brown, smooth skin salty and smokey tasting. I could feel the squeeze of his cock against my thigh as I kissed and licked down his throat and across the curving expanse of his chest. His nipples were round and hard and he squirmed and moaned as I sucked them, working the lumps of meat between my lips and flicking them with my tongue.

"Yeah, suck my tits, Mark. Christ, that feels nice. Love it when somebody works my nipples for me. You feel good on me, man. Gotta sweet, hard body. Didn't think I'd go for this but I'm feelin' too good. Lick me all over, get me wet for ya, man."

I ran my tongue up under the round crest of his pec and up along the tender side of his chest to his armpit, the sweat lush and steaming, the black hairs curling and damp as I sucked the skin down and teased him. Manny was humping his cock against my thigh and his arms were nearly crushing my back as he held me tight against his powerful torso, his round, brown face clenched and eyes shut as he mumbled and groaned above me.

Licking along the tight grooves of his buckled stomach, I edged nearer to his cock, the fat head still wrapped in a thick hood of skin, the tip glistening with come. Spreading his bulky legs wide, I crouched between them and touched his balls with the tip of my tongue feeling them twitch and jump as they drew nearer the base. His balls were almost hairless, the skin slick and glossy against my tongue as I gathered them into my mouth. Manny wrapped his legs around my head and squeezed, his back arching and his fingers rolling the tip of his cock.

Holding his thighs up, I bent my head down under his balls and licked at the thick wad of skin behind leading to his asshole, the trail edged with coarse black hairs, goosebumps rising on his thighs as I rubbed my mouth back into the salty crack. Spreading his legs wider and pushing, I rolled him onto his stomach and he lifted his hips up.

The skin over his square, hard cheeks was a honey brown, smooth and clefted, the seam dark down the center. Fitting my thumbs between, I pulled it open slightly and touched my tongue to the sweaty crease, Manny groaning and raising up against my face, his dark, bitter hole snapping open and closed as I nudged it.

"Yeah, aw, Jesus, Mark, never had nobody eatin' out my hole before. Christ, it good feelin' ya dig into me. Work me clean. Suck out my tight asshole. Stuff your tongue up side me. Work me hard. Feels so fucking good with your face up inside there."

Manny was rocking back and forth against my face, his hand behind my head and gripping me to the wet crack. His hole slowly began to loosen and I wedged the tip of my tongue inside him, worming up into his guts as I wrapped my fingers around his shaft. I could feel the come drooling down against the hard shaft and he suddenly lay flat and flipped over, his hands shoving my mouth down on his cock, impaling me as he fucked up hard against my face.

His cock was darker than the rest of his body, the thick, veiny skin soft over the hard pole. His musk rose thick as fog around my head and I opened my throat as much as I could, the fat rod rolling down over my tongue and pressing against the roof of my mouth. My jaws cracked and ached as he rammed deeper, pounding my head down and snapping his hips up until my lips were wrapped tightly around the base and the head was gouging into the back of my throat. The satiny length rode my mouth until it was soaked, meaty and broad like the rest of him, salty and fleshy with a strong spicy flavor.

When his breathing was coming back down, I pulled off his cock, dragging at the skin and swallowing as he held back from coming and sucked down his breath. Pulling to the head, I worked the thick wad of foreskin between my lips, biting and pulling it before tucking my tongue up under the flap and rolling it over the glossy purple head. Manny gripped my thigh and pulled me up, positioning my hips over his head so he could stroke and lick my dick as it dangled over his face.

"So fuckin' good, man," he gasped under me, my cock slowly sliding in and out of his mouth. "Feel so fuckin' good on my cock. Suckin' my cock down your tight throat, workin' the skin. Gotta feel it up your ass, man. Wanna feel it working out your ass."

Pulling reluctantly off his body, I pulled open the nightstand drawer and took out a condom and some lube. I tossed him the rubber and he caught it, his face blank and his breath quick and rasping as he bit into the pack and ripped it open, rolling the latex over his hard quickly. I then tossed him the lube and lay back, my hands behind my head. He opened the jar and took some on his fingers, slicking down his cock and then climbing up between my raised legs.

Kneeling above me, he looked twice as big, his puffed, meaty chest leaning over mine, his shoulders and arms bunched and rounded thickly, his black hair wet with sweat. Manny propped his cock against my balls and fucked slowly as his fingers stroked the lube against the outside of my ass gently, teasing me with the tips of his fingers.

"Gonna make ya feel nice, man. Sweet, tight hole. Ya got me so hot, worked me up 'til I don't know my name hardly. Gotta get inside your ass, man. Gotta be fuckin' up inside this hard fuckin' body of yours, man. Don't mind suckin' your cock, man, but I gotta get a feel of that ass."

"Get down and suck my wad some more, Manny," I told him as he started slowly working a finger up my ass. "Want that fat cock pumpin' my butt and that pretty face of yours eating in my lap. Gonna suck that wad for me, man? Come on, get down on it and suck me while I get loose enough to take that fat dick in me."

With a moan, Manny pressed his hairy cheek against my bloated meat and began munching it, fitting the head down between his pursed lips and letting it ride down his throat smoothly while his fingers slid between the tight ring of my ass. He sucked me down to the hairs without gagging, slurping and rocking against my gut as his fingers wriggled and rolled me loose.

Pulling back off, Manny kissed up against my stomach, wrapping his arms around my torso as he slid slowly up and lay flat over my body, his legs pinning back my thighs with his cock wedged against mine. His full lips bumped against mine, his tongue dipping down and flicking against my teeth, his head pulling my breath away as he sucked my lower lip into his mouth.

Wrapping himself tighter around my body his bulk nearly swallowed me up as his mouth fit in near my ear. "Gotta fuck ya, man. Put my cock up that ass of yours. Wanna feel you takin' that fat cock in your tight ass, suckin' this mutha down."

Reaching between us, I wrapped my fingers around his thick, hard shaft and lifted my legs on either side of his hips. Fitting the tip against my hole, I held him back, taking just an inch in and relaxing as his body shivered against mine. His beard was scraping against my throat as he groaned and begged to fuck me, his hips shaking as I slowly loosened and the sharp pains started to ease away.

Pressing my hips up, I took most of him, Manny's tough, powerful body convulsing and lifting above my chest. His cock swelled inside my guts, filling me like a balloon as he pressed down harder and deeper, the head finally punching against the insides and sending a shock of draining electricity through my nerves.

Laying back, I lifted my hips even with his and he drew out again, rocking forward with a curving swing, then slowly easing out, fucking in a long, drawn rhythm as he held his chest a breath over mine and dripped light kisses over my eyes and cheeks.

"Christ, your some tight mutha, man. Squeezin' the juice outta my balls with that hard butt of yours. Feels sweet, you wrapped around my meat, man. Never had nobody so good to me. Most of 'em wanna just suck me off, get that monster in their mouths and never let go. Ladies just want me bumpin' 'em 'til they scream blue. You wanna have me workin' ya like you workin' me. Never had such a good one. Gonna treat you right. Gonna fuck you steady and long with this man's cock. Such a fuckin' good lookin' man, feels good even suckin' on that fat dick of yours. Ain't much on shit like that but you even make that feel right."

Looking down between our bodies, I could see the firm outline of muscle flexing and hardening across our chests and stomachs. Manny slowly lifted and then lowered, the thick dark meat sliding out then coasting back between my raised legs, his smooth, dark chest over my lighter one, the thick curling bunch of hairs around the base of his cock scratching against my tight balls.

I took hold of his nipples and rubbed them, rolling the round, hard tips in my fingers before reaching out and roaming my hands over the thick, broad expanse of his torso, rubbing in the sweat that coated him. The long, thick rope of hair curled down against his throat and I pulled the rubber band away. The hair was glossy and silky as I ran my fingers through it, holding the back of his neck and pulling his face to mine.

Gripping my shoulders, Manny held me tight as his lips fastened to mine and his tongue dodged in and around my mouth. Holding me firm, he bucked his hips up, ramming his cock deep into my guts, pressing back my thighs and twisting his whole body to gouge deeper into me. He lifted with his knees and let his heavy body fall against mine over and over, fucking faster, harder, hammering into my ass, pounding the air from my lungs and slapping hard against my numbing insides.

His hard, tight ballsac was bumping the split crease of my ass, the hairs scratching and tickling against the base of my cock as he punched into me with curving, scooping thrusts, his fingers winding around my arms until I ached, his sweaty, musky body turning slick as it humped and squirmed over mine.

"Gonna come, man," he started gasping as he rabbit kicked his dick through my tight hole. "Gonna dump this load way up that tight, steamin' ass of yours. Christ, you're rippin' my balls apart, man. Gonna blow up inside ya, man, gonna come deep in that hard butt of yours, man."

Pulling out suddenly, Manny flipped over and yanked me across his gut, his fingers flashing over his hard, greasy meat. My hard cock flopped between the rounded, twin mounds over his chest and he squeezed them tight around my shaft.

"Jack that fucker off over my chest, man," he said with short breaths. "Wanna feel ya dump your load on me when I come. Wanna feel ya get off on me."

Shoving a pair of fingers back up my ass, Manny rammed and

twisted them as I leaned back and started jacking off, his own hand bumping the small of my back as his eyes stared at me getting off. A searing blue flame was burning between my balls as his fingers wrenched my guts, his handsome, tough body between my legs sweaty and dark.

Riding his fingers, I felt his hard body contract under me and the come rip from my balls, shooting out in long arcs that splashed across the bed and down across his throat and chest, the come surging up and coating him, mixing with the sweat over his body and dripping down between the deep grooves of his taut muscle.

I could feel Manny's body stiffen under mine when I shot off, the warm, wet streaks slapping over my back. He pulled his fingers from my ass and wiped the come over his body as he bucked and twisted, his come dripping down against my spine and puddling over his stomach.

Reaching up, he pulled my body down over his, his warm, slick lips sliding over mine as we lay numbed with exhaustion, his hands gliding across my back and wiping his come into me, our bodies becoming sticky with drying come and sweat.

"Christ, man," he sighed and then laughed. "Ya done me better than I could. Been wantin' to try a man for a while. Something I've always wanted. Just didn't find the guy 'til you. Ain't that something ?" His hand was wrapped around my cock, stroking and tugging it gently, his lips brushing my face as he talked lazily. Taking my hand, he held it between his strong legs and lifted them so I could feel the damp crease of his ass and the wrinkled hole. "Something to look forward to," he whispered in my ear.

CREAMED MARINE

RICK JACKSON

I FUCKED MY FIRST MARINE back in '79. Back then I was a naive bootcamp passing through Subic Bay on my first cruise around the Pacific. I'd gone out with my buddies and watched them screw whores to pool tables, but bar sluts didn't interest me. What inflated my crank was the sight of those thick sailor dicks drilling away, sliding in and out of tight holes. The craving that those hard, glistening ramrods might find a target closer to home became the waking fantasy I could not escape. Two days later, when I stopped by the crapper at the Spanish Gate snack bar to dump and pump a couple of loads to ease my frustration, I was ready for love.

Kent's scrawled call to action was as simple as it was effective:

19-year-old carnivorous marine
needs creamy meat bad
2200 15SPT Sp Gate.

That night was both the 15th and my last free night in port, so you can bet your pension I was leaning against the Gate when Kent tooled up in his car. He let the motor purr while his eyes slid up and down along my body like a glutton with a free meal pass. I couldn't see much of Kent until the door swung open, but I saw enough. He looked like a blond, green-eyed version of Ricky Nelson from the chin up and like a Greek god from the neck down. I was ready, but neither of us said a word as we rolled through the night. We didn't have to. As I slid my fingers up towards the crotch of his cut-offs, the gooseflesh they found covering his hard thigh spoke volumes. I was too struck by his power and classic marine-quality beauty to worry where he was going. Halfway to Cubi, he turned off the main road and pulled up by the base riding stables. The slut had clearly done this before.

When he eased out of the car and stood glowing in the moonlight, I was impressed with how compact he was. Only about 5'8", he had battalion-strength muscles packed into every savory inch of that height. I decided he would do, even if he wasn't a virgin.

His hand found mine to lead me up to a pile of hay in the corner between the corral fence and the stable building. My crank was already trying to rip a hole out of my trou, but when I felt his hand slide along my flanks, so much blood rushed to my heads that I nearly passed out. His fingers eased up under my t-shirt and around into the sweaty small of my back. Kent's marine biceps contracted to pull my body against his as his lips found mine. Our lips and tongues slithered and sucked as the scent of his body blended together with the hay and horseshit and the jungle smells wafting down the hill. My guts turned rapidly to mush under the delicious abuse of his hands and tongue, but one secret corner of my brain kept working well enough to teach me what having a man could be like.

Looking back, I have no memory of how we got naked. I suppose my life-long need for love and the feel of Kent's tongue and lips and hands slithering across my sweaty flesh must have fused every circuit I had. I only know that when I broke away from him for a moment to catch my breath and admire, I saw the moonlight sparkling off hard, bare muscle. His lizard throbbed, thick and ready against his belly ; his balls hung low and heavy between hard thighs. Kent's chest heaved as he struggled for air, his passion-pointed tits fucking the night air as a stream of sweat trickled down across his belly to disappear into his golden pubes. He was the most perfect thing I'd ever seen in my life : a flawless young animal in heat — and all mine.

Even back then I had already heard how marines liked to be treated. I somehow found the strength to break the spell woven by his perfection and the tropical moonlight — and, most of all, by my gut-wrenching need for his body. "OK, marine," I barked, "On your knees. You need meat bad ? Eat this, cocksucker." He slipped to his knees on the straw ; my hands grabbed him hard behind his close-cropped head. My dick, swollen to a thickness it had never known before, slammed hard against his cheek and started prodding at his mouth until I'd fucked my way inside. In the years since, I've refined my technique, making sure the dude gives my lizard a slow basting before I ream out his gullet, but that night nothing could have held me back. My hips swung my body forward, cramming my eight thick inches of naval pride through Kent's mouth and down into his throat. When I looked down to savor the sight of his perfect male body hanging off my joint, I saw his cat-green eyes fucked open in surprise as my rod raped his throat. My hands around his cute little ears started twisting his head slightly so I could literally screw myself down his throat. My little marine love-monkey gagged and choked, but kept his hands tight on station around my butt so he couldn't cough himself off my joint. I pulled my dickhead out of his mouth to give him a second's breath — and to have the delicious feel of his throat grinding backwards along my trigger-ridge. Once I felt his tongue lapping and lashing the length of my lizard, I twisted his face back down where it belonged, screwing his nose into my stiff red pubes. As I got down to serious facefucking, I moved one hand to the back of his head and slid the other over his hard marine body. Stroking him like the fine animal he was, I let my fingers glide across his wrestler-quality neck and down lower across his massive shoulders until I found the stallion-like muscles of his back. The feel of my balls slamming into his strong chin, the wet love of my dick down his throat, the sound of soft slurps and modest chokes as he worked between my legs all combined together to satisfy me almost as much as shooting my load down his throat. When I looked down again at the gorgeous face impaled on my meat, his eyes were shut, savoring his pleasure. Kent was playing with my nuts with one hand as he stoked my pole, but was still kneading my ass with the other — almost as much as I needed his. The cocksucker's hunky charm and serious suction had pulled my load up into the firing chamber. I knew I'd spooge the back of his head off if I kept my pole down his hole another minute.

I had long since learnt that marines crave nothing more than abuse so I snarled, "Bitch! Where did you learn to suck cock? Suck dick like a man or spit it out." I gave him an especially vicious jab with my joint and knocked his ass backwards onto the hay. When he looked up at me with his hungry, tomcat eyes, I made his day: "That's right, grunt. Show me how you marines love to lick ass." I turned tail and leaned against the upper rail of the corral, arching my ass upward slightly so he could work his cute little pug nose up my butt. Kent slid his hands around my thighs as he nosed his way between the hard muscles of my squid ass. He prodded at my hole for a moment like a hog snuffling for truffles. I felt his tongue lash out like a spaniel's, slick-sliding along the trench on the way toward my shithole. That tongue skipped around my pucker for a moment, half teasing, half getting a feel for the neighborhood. My pink pucker twitched and shuddered under his tongue-lashing. Then, when he dropped down to drill deep into my butthole, I felt myself clench up tight, locking him inside me. Incredibly, his lips encircled my hole so he could suck my pucker at the same time he was tongue-fucking me. His nose and jaw smeared themselves against my ass-crack, trying to pry my cheeks far enough apart so he could get his whole face up my butt. As I leaned against the weathered wood of the corral in the moonlight, one shiver after another swept up my spine as that buttlicking marine chowed down. His hands pulled me harder into his greedy snout with every flick of his tongue. Nothing shuts my brain down faster than a rimming; Kent's marine tongue all but put me into a coma. My whole world lay up my ass. Every nerve I had seemed to itch and be instantly scratched by his fluttering, drilling tongue until I felt myself slip into the kind of brainlock where time stands still and all you know is the pleasure up your butt. Somehow, moments or centuries later, I came to again to find him happier than ever. Loud, butt-muffled snorts and slurps and groans of pleasure soared out into the moonlit night. I took stock and decided that my load had oozed back down out of firing position. My dick told me that as much fun as my butthole was having, it was time to ream some serious marine ass.

Getting with the plan wasn't easy, though. I finally had to reach back and use both hands to pry Kent off my shithole. By the time I turned around, he was licking his lips and looking as though I'd taken away his last crust of bread. I got him even more turned on, if that were possible, by saying he couldn't kiss ass any better than he could suck dick — so he should assume the position and show me whether he could at least take what I have like a man. A grin flashed across his face and he hopped to his feet, bent double, and grabbed his ankles like a high school student in the dean's office. My dick had never felt so ready, so swollen the skin of my crankshaft threatened to split open with every throb of my racing heart. I stood again, just admiring his body. The moonlight gave the scene a dreamlike quality as his handsome, hard, hairless flesh seemed to gleam and shimmer before me. I memorized every curve of skin and tight ripple of muscle so that some day, when I am old and want to remember what youth was about, I can think back on Kent and, for a moment, be young again.

He needed it bad and grew restless being raped by nothing more substantial than my gaze. I'm not usually a romantic. I generally bend the guy over, hump butt, shoot, and move on. Kent's marine body was so impossibly perfect that somehow I knew I would never have anything better. If this was going to be the fuck of my life, I was going to ream him right.

I growled that I was still waiting — for him to get on his back like the slut he was and lift his legs. He slid down to the pile of straw and spread wide. I raised his head for a moment and shoved it down my dick, warning him that his spit was all the lube he was going to get. He drooled across my dickhead and gave me another Wally-Cleaver smile as he said something about not wanting me to be too slick. He wanted it rough and raw. His massive calves wrapped around the small of my back ; his heels spurred my butt, begging me to ride him long and hard. As he slid his hands upward along my flanks to grip my shoulders, I felt him tremble like a bootcamp in a whorehouse.

I put my face above his, reaching down for a moment to brush his lips with mine. His eyes shone through to his soul, begging for what was coming, savoring the moment, and sharing my pleasure at being young men in lust. He grinned that goofy grin marines have, and we both knew it was time. I felt his butt grasping at my bone and eased against his fuckhole where his tender tissues fluttered and nibbled at my cum-slit like a sheep in clover. I was almost afraid to slam my thick dick up into his eager marine butt and ruin the perfection of anticipation. No human could live up to the impossible expectations I'd formed.

Kent's tight marine butt did, though. He was so tight, in fact, that I had to ram my rod against his fuckhole three times before he was able to open enough. The minute I finally slammed into the tight, slick warmth of his government-owned ass, I discovered he was even better than I'd expected. His satin-soft shitchute rippled up and down along my crankshaft like a troop of tap-dancing millipedes. Like everything else he had, his prostate was man-sized — and bounced off my diving dork like a nugget of pure pleasure. As I'd ripped into his butt, his delicious green eyes slammed shut in fulfillment and his mouth gaped open, trying to suck in enough air to extinguish the fire in his guts. As soon as I finished my first brutal, triumphant stroke of conquest and felt my hard dickhead pricking the very end of his fuck-tunnel, he opened his eyes with a sparkle. They shone in gratitude and satisfaction. Most marines don't feel whole unless they have it up the ass ; Kent was no exception.

Once I finished grinding my stiff red pubes into the straining rim of his fuckhole, I warned my marine mount to hold tight for the ride of his life. I started off slowly enough, letting his guts slide up my shaft on their own as his hips arched upward to meat me. He climbed my pole as though it were a spiral staircase, using my swollen dickhead to scrape away at his guts on the way in. The ankles parked on my ass urged me ever lower, ever harder, ever faster. Soon I was humping away in earnest, letting my hips and the most basic instinct of our species count my cadence. My waist curled inward like a lobster's tail as I arced harder with every vicious, demanding thrust, driving my eight thick inches of naval weapon far enough up Kent's writhing ass to satisfy even him. As I picked up speed, the SLAPs and THWACKs of my hips slamming into his hard butt were drowned out by Kent's grunts as I drove my point home and soft, almost subsonic moans as I pulled everything but my dickhead out of him. Now and again, just to teach his ass humility, I popped all the way out and slid my dick along his sweaty ass-crack. When I got tired of jerking myself off with his ass, I'd arch up again and ram back down into him, breaking his butt open all the wider. As the sounds of our bodies humping together and our mutual moans and grunts of satisfaction grew louder, I slipped back into the fugue of mindless animal pleasure I'd felt with his tongue up my butt. I remember sliding my hands across his massive hairless pecs to play with his iron-hard tits, tweaking and twisting them like dials on a radio as though I were trying to tune his moans of terrible pleasure in even better. I remember feeling my belly slam into his cum-choked ballbag and pound his dick. Most of all, though, I remember his smell as my face slipped down toward his so I could nuzzle his neck like a newborn foal on a cool spring morning. He smelt of sweat and straw and man. His tongue twisted and fluttered in my ear, driving me right to the brink as I did him hard up the ass.

I came too soon, of course. When you fuck someone as fine as Kent, it's impossible to get enough. I remember coming to as the last of my creamy jism jetted up into his ass to soothe the dick-burn which had spread its golden ecstasy throughout both our bodies. Even then, at 23, I knew I was living the high-point of my life. I would go on to other men and drop other loads, but no single experience could approach what I felt for — and inside — Kent that moonlit night.

We kept doing the nasty, of course. When I finally pulled my dick out into the night air to let our juices dry for awhile, I sucked his beautiful uncut dick. I love 'skins and would have kept him down my throat all night. Unfortunately, between the general excitement of being reamed out and the particular pleasure my dick slapped out of his prostate, his 19-year-old marine meat didn't stand a chance. I had only nursed him for a minute or so before I got a throatful of cream. I looked up about halfway through his load to see every muscle in his body knotted in pleasure as his hips exploded upward into my face. His hands on my head felt at home, as though we had been together always — perhaps in another life. When I'd drained the last drop of his prime quality USMC Grade-A man-milk, I straddled his head and sat roughly on his face. He licked my butthole and balls and everything else I put within reach until it was time for me to do him again. The next time, I did stand him up against the barn so I could play with his dick and tits while I gave him an extra-large asshole. By morning we were so sore and happy from pleasuring each other that we could only manage to drag our dicks back to the car. I had duty that day and we pulled out of Subic early the next, so I never came across Kent again. In the years since, I have been happy, but as I snuggle up to my current squeeze in the middle of the night, I often wonder where the marines and fate have taken Kent since that single, perfect fulfilling night a dozen years ago. A man knows many things at 34 that eluded him at 23. I see now, of course, that if I had stayed in touch, we might have made a life together.

On the other hand, there's something special about your first marine. Maybe it is just as well he can live forever — unchanging, unaging, and perfect beyond words — trapped like a fly in moonlit amber.

READY FOR ACTION

RICK JACKSON

T HAT GOOD FRIDAY AFTERNOON in 1981, I wasn't looking
for a good time when I went into the crapper at LAX ; I was
looking for a place to tap a kidney. I'd seen the marine hordes,
of course. They were hard to miss, streaming out of the international terminal with their duffel bags and savory muscles. It's
hard for even me to think about tight marine butt, though, when
I'm about to explode a piss-grenade inside one of America's bus-
iest airports. Still, when I popped through the door and saw
Daren standing there, naked but for the jumper that didn't begin
to cover his ass, I couldn't help noticing how choice he was. That
classic marine butt hanging out from under with its two teeth-
tingling mounds of manmuscle just waiting to be skewered by my
thick nine inches of naval armament made me take notice. Sometimes a guy's just got to put personal pain aside in the pursuit of
art. I kept my feet moving toward the pisser, but the image of that
cute little body of his flashed into my consciousness like a nova
in a coal mine. As I stood there, staring at the wall and feeling one
sort of relief surge from my dick as a fierce gusher of steamy piss
splashed down the drain, the image of that muscle-packed ass
thrusting out from under his olive-drab jumper naturally began
to prey on my mind. I'd only gotten a glance at his face before my
eyes focused on his butt, but that was enough. He was blond and
fresh and looked as shocked as if I'd just shat on his grand-
mother. When he saw I didn't intend to molest him just then, he
went back to looking through his duffel for the civilian pants he
wanted to put on. That hard, hairless ass wouldn't leave me
alone, though. I hadn't had anything warm wrapped around my
dick in nearly a dozen hours — and hadn't reamed marine butt in
over a week. As I gave my drained lizard a shake, I felt him leap,
instinctively ready for action. When I glanced back over my
shoulder, young Daren was wearing jeans but had lost the jumper. His chest and belly were as hairless as his butt had been —
and just as tasty-looking. The tiled chill of the crapper made his
tits stand out hard and rosy and firm and ready. I don't normally

molest men in public johns; when you're a good-looking sailor, you don't need to cruise bus stations. Daren was just exceptional enough for me to make an exception.

I shook it off and then left my lizard dangling out of my pants as I turned around and used as nonchalant a voice as I could find to say, "If you men just got back to the States, I'll bet you'd like your butt reamed out by something hard and thick." Just putting my feelings into words made my dick start to come to attention. I saw Daren look up, ready to snarl; but when he saw me standing there in my dress whites, gold wings gleaming on my chest, with my man-sized meat bouncing up and down in time with my racing heart, he just dropped his cute little mouth open and stared. I returned the favor and got my first long, slow look at him. His green eyes and perfect nose would have inflated my crank on an average body. One glance at his denim-clad basket and the hard, hairless torso just feet away convinced me that even if I didn't ream his butt then, I'd remember his hot young body for jerk-off material for months to cum.

Marines aren't usually accused of being quick thinkers. As his eyes savored every pulse of my dick, I felt it rise to pound against my belly, ready for action. When he finally stammered something, I knew he was mine. Marines talk tough, but most of them love nothing better than to have squid dick up their butts. The fact I was an officer — and pretty much of a stud myself — made the temptation irresistible. My only regret was that my ship was due to leave in two hours. Young Lance Corporal Daren Barker, USMC had the kind of body you wanted to use slowly, again and again over a week-end or a week or a lifetime. Still, if all we had time for was a quick fuck in the toilet, I was going to make sure the kid never forgot what a sailor could do with his joy-stick.

I gave him a *Top-Gun* grin and nodded towards the end crapper. He followed me in, leaving his duffle bag just outside where he could keep an ear on it. Since my cock was already crowing, I pushed his ass down onto the seat and shoved the thickest joint he'd sucked all day smack into his mouth. He had the face of a bootcamp, but sucked dick like a sergeant major. His wet tongue slithered across the throbbing head of my dick to moisten my meat and then darted deep into my cum-slit. His lips slathered spit across my head as they worked to catch up to the tongue and engulfed every raw nerve in my cock like the dictionary illustration of a good time. I half felt his hands cupping my ass through my whites, but that studly young face held my attention as it worked its way over my trigger-ridge and down my crankshaft. My dick was harder than shit on a stick, but the kid managed to pull it down far enough to work it back into the very depths of his throat. Once he had me where I wanted me, he clamped down with the tight, tender tissues of his expert cock-sucking throat and started getting friendly. As his suction level slid up through "max" to "overdrive," his tongue fluttered along the bottom of my shaft. That throat was a marvel. At the same time he was sucking, he was able to grind his soft throat muscles along my head, tantalizing a new nerve cluster with each blazing stroke until I began to feel as though my best asset were caught in a milking machine from hell. I heard myself moaning and realized that my hips had found their ancient, driving rhythm. My hands were on the foxy close-cropped head at my crotch as I pivoted and rammed and torqued my bone down Daren's insatiable, dick-licking facehole.

He must have helped me with my belt and pants, because I noticed that they were around my ankles and his fingers were prying my ass apart, sliding seductively along my crack, looking for a good time. At one point, he pulled one hand out and smelt it as he kept cadence on my cock. Hard as it was with my meat down his throat, I could almost see the kid smile. My hands moved to his ears and I found myself ramming harder and deeper into his face, carelessly fucking him as hard as I could like the beautiful sex-object he was. When my hips took control of our destiny, I lost track of the world and drifted off into the splendid oblivion that comes to men only when they're using what they have to the fullest. The harder I slammed my dick down Daren's throat, the harder he sucked and the farther I drifted away toward ecstasy. He must have put his hands back on my butt, because I suddenly felt my balls erupt with blast after gut-wrenching blast of their white fury. Later, I felt his fuckfingers prying my shithole apart, but just then all I knew was that ten million electron volts seemed to be coursing through my cock. The combination of his cock-torture and expert fingerwork was too much for any twelve-hour virgin to withstand. I came more or less back to earth to find my cock pounding so far down his hot, marine throat that it should have come out his asshole. The last few spurts of my spooge splashed down into his guts and I felt the satisfaction of a job well done.

He must have sensed my recovery, because the greedy thing pried his face off my dickhead and slid me back out into his mouth where his tongue went at my desperate dick like a lawn mower, whirling about my super-tender meat until every nerve exploded again in the frenzied fuck-fury of a lifetime. I felt more jism jolt up from somewhere to jet out against the back of his mouth. I tried to pull his ears back so I could escape, but he wasn't going to be satisfied until I was drier than Nefertiti's grandfather. Once a jarhead gets an idea in his mind, there's no getting it out again. I just clenched my teeth and held on while he sucked my bone dry.

In a way I was pissed. I'd planned to dump my first load of the afternoon up his butt. He'd sucked so much out of me, I wouldn't be able to do a body like his justice for several minutes. Once he finally let my lizard escape, licking his lips and looking up at me with worshipful green eyes, I told him to stand up and drop trou. He'd unbuttoned them while he was working on me, but I couldn't see much. As I took his place on the crapper and that gorgeous uncut marine meat slid into view, I knew it was worth the wait. His foreskin was so big and floppy that even with his dick pounding hard and ready against his hairless belly, there was still enough 'skin left over to make a frilly crown around his cum-slit. Like most men, I've never been able to get enough uncut meat. Daren's wasn't quite as long as mine, but was every bit as thick — and with that 'skin, I'd have traded tools in a minute. I looked up at him and the goofy kid blushed and asked if it was good enough. I told him it would do for now. Marines really can be precious.

I slipped my lips around his man-sized nuts, slurping one and then the other into my mouth for some good old-fashioned jaw-breaking fun. The long hours he had spent on his flight had filled his crotch with the best smell in the world: man musk. As I worked on his nuts, running my tongue across their hard surfaces until he winced, playing with his sperm-bag, and otherwise being mischievous, I filled my lungs with the glorious scent of his manhood. My teeth ached to get hold of that gorgeous dick, but that sweaty, musky smell made me do something I had done only once before. I finished playing with his balls, spat them out, and ordered him to face front. If his balls stank of man, the beautiful marine butt was fly-boy heaven on earth.

A first, I just admired the thing. You don't spend six years in the Navy without seeing asses, but this was a Renaissance masterpiece of butts. His cheeks were completely hairless, for one thing — and covered in the softest skin you can imagine. Underneath, though, his muscles were hard and firm without a hint of the slack-assed droop so many otherwise well-built men have. These huge cheeks jutted straight out from his hips, proud and perfect — floating as though by magic, just waiting for my buttbuster to teach them new tricks. I spread them apart and told Daren to bend over. The cleft was even better than perfect. His crack was moist and sweaty from his flight, but smooth and hairless as an impure thought. My nose slid between his silken mounds of marine manmuscle and stole great lungfuls of his glory. I sniffed lower and deeper, scooping his hard flesh away with my nose and, finally, reached his beautiful pink pucker. It pulsed in time with his passion like the temporary portal to another, more perfect dimension. My tongue darted across his tender flesh, flicking here and there to tantalize his ass and keep him from knowing what to expect. Soon, though, I was tongue-fucking his ass, delving deep down between those perfect pink folds to rape the motherlode of his sweaty marine manmusk. My lips worked their way around his hole so I could suck as well as tongue and soon my soul was drenched in his immaculate, incredibly sensational taste and smell and presence. My hands clawed at his butt to spread his muscles wider so I could get more of my face against his ass. I ignored his groans and moans of pleasure as my tongue tore deep down into his fuckhole and dug up every molecule of his essence within reach. His ass ground into my face, but soon even that wasn't good enough and I had to admit I needed a longer organ to do his meaty marine ass justice. Fortunately for us both, I had just the tool.

I eased my face away from his hole and was about to prong the living shit out of him when I remembered that dick. If his cock tasted anything like his ass, I needed it bad. I spun him around for a moment to discover that his crown of cock-skin was flooded with clear, sticky pre-cum. His flow was so thick that it had over-flowed his head and dribbled down the thick shaft of his dick. My tongue blended one of nature's gifts with another as his musk slid into that stream of pre-cum. I slurped up the overflow and eased my lips around his plum-sized dickhead. At first, I could get all I could handle by sucking lightly ; but soon I had to pry his treas-ure out with my tongue, sliding it deep down between the baby-soft 'skin and the purple, passion-pulsing dickmeat hidden below. His lizard was more than enough to keep me busy for a lifetime, but I couldn't resist letting my hands caress his hard pecs and grind my palms into the rosy, passion-tipped tits that crowned each of them. I let one hand slither down across his washboard belly and travel up his flanks. He shivered his ap-preciation of my handiwork and began thrusting his dick harder into my face. As my lizard-licking tongue slid around inside his cocksock, I felt his body quake a Richter 8.0 and knew he was about to blow the biggest gusher of USMC Grade-A prime in history straight into my face. I did what any brave sailor would have done under the same circumstances : I gripped his dick hard around the throat and slammed his skin downward, stripping back his 'skin and leaving his sensitive knob undefended. My tongue started to whirl around his tortured flesh like a dervish in a whirlwind, sending shocks and shivers down his crankshaft to explode his weapon into enough action to satisfy a battalion. Just as the first salvo was fired, I slipped both my fuckfingers into the hole my tongue had lately left and started prying his ass open. I knew the exercise would not only blow the top of his fucking head off when he came, but Daren would need to be opened up if I was going to get my dick up inside his ass. There was no time like the present. The instant my fingers slid inside his fuckhole, the first glob of sweet, creamy cock-snot blew up into my mouth and proved beyond doubt that marines keep more than one unforgettable taste about them. When the second wave hit a split second and cock-thrust later, I found I didn't have room for his jism and his dick both. Unwilling to lose either, I slid part of his dick out of my mouth but kept my spooge-slicked lips sliding up and down across his tender dickhead while I sucked and scraped and teased my whip-tailed little jarhead recruit up out of his overloaded ballbag.

I was so busy chugging down his perfect, pure protein that I only heard part of what he was saying. It was all senseless jarhead stuff about "Oh, yessss, Jesus . . . Shhhittttt, yeeesssss. . . ." so I didn't much listen. Soon, I couldn't keep up with his stream of cream and had to slam my face down his dork. Grinding my nose into his soft pubes, I was able to let him inject his protein straight down into my guts. I stayed put, his spooge-spunking cock pulsing wide, stretching my throat out of shape, until I heard his moans taper off — about the time I started to pass out from lack of air. When his dickhead slid back into my mouth, I gave him one or two quick wipes to tidy up the dribbles, but that was it. I had waited long enough.

Before he could even begin to recover full consciousness, I spun his ass around and shoved my dick up into his tight marine butt. He let out a squeal, but it was immediately followed by a groan of ecstasy that roared up from his very depths. I slammed his head into the the door of the stall and let my hips pound their passion straight up into that gorgeous ass. My hands reached down, first to his shoulders and then to his tits. I grabbed one in each hand and used them almost like reins as I rode his ass hard and deep and fast. I'd just been tapped out twenty minutes before so I knew I had a little time to enjoy his lean young body. His slick shit-chute slid along my crankshaft like a summer's mist, soft yet hot, soothing yet stimulating. Daren was using every foul word the Corps had taught him as he panted and heaved on the end of my dick, taking everything I had and loving the abuse. I knew he'd like me to rag his ass, so I yelled shit about how all marines were faggot-assed pansies and none of them could take squid dick like men. I couldn't give him all the verbal abuse he craved, though ; I was too busy reaming his tight young butt.

He had been in the Corps long enough to become a lance corporal, so I was sure he'd had dozens of men before me up his ass ; but it had obviously been awhile. He was tighter than Scrooge and louder than fuck, moaning and swearing and pounding on the stall of the door while I rammed and torqued and drilled his butt. I leaned forward to nibble at his ear lobe and then, when I saw how much he liked that, I tongue-fucked him to shivers, drilling my hot wet organ into yet another hole. My breath gushed back out of his ear at me, a ferocious animal snarl that proved civilization and fucking don't mix. I was raping his ass by right of conquest. He craved everything I had, but just then I didn't care — I used him as my whore, just the way he wanted to be taken. I felt my dickhead ricochet off his prostate and slam relentlessly into the blind end of his fuck-tunnel. My stiff rust-colored pubes ground into his shattered asshole and still my dick wasn't happy. Losing my first load down his throat had been a blessing. Under normal circumstances, I would have blown my bilges after thirty or forty fuck-thrusts this wild. As it was, I pronged his ass until we both lost count and bucked on cross-country like the wild stallions we were. My teeth finally locked onto the back of his neck like some jungle cat and I felt my guts flush up through my piston-driven dick to explode creamy shrapnel that blew apart any lingering barriers between us. My teeth gripped his neck, my hands held tight onto his tits, and my dick tore its proud victory into Daren's tight marine foxhole. I gushed and pounded and twisted and spunked until I thought my heads would come off.

When I finally came back to my senses, I'd fucked Daren up against the stall door and overflowed his butt. My airdale spooge had splattered back onto my balls and thighs and made a mess of Daren's beautiful behind. When I couldn't dry-hump him another lick, I collapsed backwards onto the crapper and gasped for air. He moved backwards, too, still swearing and still half-drunk with orgasmic pleasure. I managed to lick a few of my jism-splatters off his ass before he collapsed into my lap. I held his ass there, sitting on my dick until the heat and contact with his marine butt got me hard again. By the time I'd nailed him a second time, they'd called final boarding for my flight and I had to run ; but you can believe I gave him my number before I tore out. You can also believe that when I got back to Long Beach two weeks later, the tightest ass in the United States Marine Corps was waiting on my stoop, ready for more inter-service action.

RIO DE SEMEN

RICK JACKSON

HIS SHITHOLE WRAPPED ITSELF around my dick like a wet-dream come true. His butt was so perfect I had the uneasy feeling that maybe I was just dreaming. I'm not the kind of guy who normally falls into the clover this deep and sweet. That's what that tight ass of his was, though : pure fucking clover. His olive-skinned mounds of man-muscle were soft and hairless on the outside, but packed hard and precious as marble on the inside. The dark, secret crack down his ass was even better. My lust-struck tongue had slid slowly along and felt his butt wriggle hard against my face in satisfaction. I'd had to use both hands to pry his muscle out of the way ; but my nose and chin finally won out, and I was able to use my tongue on the perfect pink pucker that he kept hidden away. The first time my tongue tip had sailed across his fuckhole, I felt his butt shiver and flutter — and then a convulsion of satisfaction wracked his whole body as though I'd shoved a high tension cable up his ass. He'd moaned something in Portuguese and gone limp as his body around his fuckhole and only strafing down into his pink passion-pit when I wanted to fuck with him. The more I teased him, though, the louder he moaned and swore in Portuguese — so the more I pronged my tongue directly into his tight, horny asshole. Within minutes, I had my lips locked around his fuckhole, sealing him up solid so I could suck at his butt while I tongue-fucked his ass. That had gotten him going something chronic. His butt flew up and tried to wrap itself around my head, squirming and writhing against my face while I worked him over. My hands were able to slide up across his hot, hunky body — across the furry, washboard belly, up along those gorgeous lats to cup his massive, pecs with their passion-pointed crowns.

As I reamed his butt with my tongue, I let my fingers play with his soft, chestnut-colored fur. His arms and legs and ass were almost completely hairless. I couldn't figure where he got that perfect pelt, so thick and incredibly masculine on his chest and belly. He was like a beautiful freak of nature, hand-crafted with me in mind. When my hands tired of his fur, I moved to torment his tits. They peaked high above his fur on twin pillars of passion-pumped purple. Every twist and torque brought a new, more delicious shudder or moan or groan until I was having almost as much fun with my hands as I was with my mouth. Eduardo was enjoying himself, too; but the greedy Latin slut still wanted more. He wanted my thick eight inches of yanqui fury up his tight Brazilian ass. The first time he begged me to fuck him, I just twisted his tits harder. I was having too good a time tongue-raping his ass and chowing down on his delicious man-musk to pull my face away from the trough. The more I worked him over, the wider my tongue pried his butt open, the more my mouth watered his hot ass, the more the needed me up his butt. Finally, I pulled away from his shithole and told the foxy little bastard that if he wanted my dick, he'd have to roll over. There was no way I was going to ram everything I had up his hole without being able to watch his face while I did him.

It had been his face that had attracted me first. I love hunky butts, but nothing pumps my 'nads like a cute, studly face. I had just gotten off the ship at the fleet landing in Rio about five minutes before. He was standing at the bus stop right outside the gate as the bus pulled up. Since he was the first guy in a Brazilian naval uniform I'd seen, I gave him and it a long look. I thought the little flat-topped hat looked stupid, but nothing could spoil my view of that gorgeous mug of his. He looked nothing like what I'd expected South Americans to look like. He looked Greek or Italian: olive skin, savory green eyes, a cute little pug nose, and that gorgeous curly brown hair. My eyes slid down to check out the rest of his body and weren't disappointed. The lizard line seemed to trace down his left thigh forever, and the way his butt jutted straight out from his hips, proud and hard and begging for what I had, promised an even better time. When he climbed aboard the bus, flashing that Tom-Cruise smile of his, and asked if I was off the Enterprise, I knew Big Rick was in fucking love. We were at a motel he knew before you could say "Copacabana."

Those green eyes gleamed up at me as I slid his thighs around my waist and used my butt-buster to pry his glorious, tight man-cheeks apart. My lizard slid into his passion-pit and waited, unwilling to break through his fuckhole just yet. I saw his tongue flick out across his lips — whether out of fear or lust or impatience, I couldn't tell and was past caring. Just hovering above him, letting my eyes wander across the hard, lean, incredibly macho body trapped beneath me had inflated my crank better than anything in a long time. I let the moment of anticipation stretch into a minute or more, knowing deep down in my guts that really raping his ass wouldn't be as much fun as the anticipation. I was wrong.

When I poked through, nudging slightly harder with every thrust of my hips against his epic ass until we both got what we wanted, I saw his gorgeous green eyes clench shut in momentary misery or celebration. His breath seized up for a minute, but when his jaw unclenched and he started gasping in air, those eyes opened to beam up at me in complete fucking contentment. I let my dick do its duty and more or less hung on for the ride. My shaft knew its way down his satin-slick shit-chute, parting his tender walls with my angry butt-buster, glancing off his prostate just for the fun of tormenting his ass, and drilling ever deeper and harder into the tight end of his love tunnel. Once my dick was on autopilot, I concentrated on sucking at those Latin lounge-lizard lips of his and letting my tongue slide along his. My hands kept at his tits for a while, but things quickly got hectic enough that I just dug in my elbows and knees and toes and let nature take its course. My forearms ended up along his flanks so I had no trouble moving my upper-body around to nip at his neck or suck his ear-lobe. The slut was grunting away like a Tijuana whore on pay-day weekend; but when I drilled my tongue into his ear, he went ape-shit. If I hadn't had him pinned tight at both ends, there's no telling what the crazy son-of-a-bitch would have done. His hands clutched at my hair, pulling my face down harder against him until I felt my flesh smear into his. I licked behind his ear and tasted the man-sweat that fueled my fuck-frenzy even further. The harder my hips pounded my dick down his tight fuck-hole, the harder and fiercer I needed to have him.

He'd started off as a studly hunk I wanted to have fun with, but something about his body was too good. Something about the noise he was making and the way he was grinding away underneath my body — the intensity of his lust was so strong that we went beyond simple fucking. I usually at least pretend to care about what my fuck-buddies want. I won't say I'm Alan Alda or the sensitive '90's type, but it's only good manners to help the guy dangling off your dick have a good time, too. With Eduardo, though, I suddenly discovered I didn't give a shit whether he was happy or not. He was mine. I had him. That was all that counted. I was going to use his butt until I'd fucked the meat from my bone — and then I might just ream his ass some more on general principles.

The rougher I fucked him, the louder he moaned and the harder his heels prodded into my ass, driving me ever farther down his shit-hole. I clamped my teeth onto his shoulder for support and then really turned my hips loose. They slammed against his tight young hole so hard that the sweaty thwack of flesh on flesh ricocheted off the walls to drown out the slut's grunts and groans. On the up-stroke, I cranked up so hard that half the time I popped my swollen dickhead clear out of his tingling ass. Now and again I'd keep it out, sliding along between those olive mounds of muscle, using his butt to jerk me off. Then my dick would catch a chill and want to go home so my hips would arc toward the ceiling and prong my joint back down through Eduardo's rapidly shrinking fuckhole. The impact and size of my dickhead would make him gasp and clench up tight with every nerve and muscle in his lust-struck young body. His seizures made my trip down through all the layers of his butt-muscles all the more delicious.

I felt Eduardo's hands pulling at my shoulders and back as though asking for mercy — and begging that I not let up. Our naked, sweating bodies pounded and writhed together like the young animals we were, unguided by morality or fears. Our only need was to enjoy each other as hard and long and deep as we could. I felt every nerve in my body come alive as never before until the blood rushed in my ears and I wondered how much faster my heart could pound without exploding. Just then, I needed Eduardo's ass more than I needed life itself, so I kept reaming down into that tight, dick-hungry Latin hole with everything I had. Time blurred as one fuckthrust faded into the next, and I hammered his hole on through the afternoon. One perfect stroke led to the next until I lost all sense of myself or him or of the world and only felt the glow of our stallion-like bodies heaving on down the final stretch, doing what came naturally.

When I felt my ballbag tighten, I tried to think of anything I could to make the magic last just a second longer, but I was too far gone. I needed to juice him — juice him deep and until my balls threatened to fall off. When my guts turned inside out and I felt glob after glorious glob of sailor spooge blast up into his tight sailor butt, except for my hips I was paralysed with ecstasy. I reamed and pounded and thrust up his ass. I felt his butthole stretch the skin of my dick tighter on every down-stroke than on the last. My cock armed and fried one bone-crunching blast after another until the friction fire my dick had drilled into his butt was drowned in wave after creamy wave of prime-quality USN joint-jism. My seaman semen spunked down his hole until there wasn't room for my dick and cum, too — so every time I drilled into his ass, I felt a gusher of my own lizard-lube splatter back out onto my tight ballbag and straining thighs. My butt clenched tight, squeezing home every drop of ass-ordnance I had. Even when I'd run dry, my body kept slamming into Eduardo's sweaty, spooge-splattered ruin of a fuckhole, dry-humping his butt to show him who was in charge. All my dick knew was that it liked drilling deep and didn't want the moment to end. Unfortunately, life isn't perfect. Eventually my wind gave out and I had to collapse into the sweaty swamp of fur that covered Eduardo's torso. I felt his hard tits grind into my bear chest as his cock pulsed hot and hard against my belly. We both knew what was cumming next — but I had to catch my breath first.

Did Eduardo hold me in his arms and whisper sweet nothings in my ear? Did he scamper into the john to drag out a cool towel to wipe my brow? Did he bring me a cold beer to kick-start my body again. He did not. About fifteen seconds after my cock eased out of his shattered butthole, he'd rolled me over onto my back and was lifting my ankles toward the ceiling. His dick wasn't in my league when it came to length, but it was every bit as thick — and twice as angry now. I'd pumped half a gallon of spit up his butt while I was rimming his ass; he didn't even know the meaning of "dick-lube." Or didn't care. Those green eyes of his gleamed down at me, and his face slid open in a grin. He let one hand glide over my bare, heaving chest as sweat streamed across it — but that was more by way of anticipation than foreplay.

Now it was my turn to feel the fury of a sailor's dick up my butt, and I wasn't sure I was ready. In a way, I guess it's just as well I was exhausted. If every muscle in my young body hadn't just been worn to a frazzle, I suppose that thick dick up my butt would have really hurt. As it was, it did a pretty good imitation. I felt my ass split open as his pounding handful of manhood pronged through my virtue and he used me like a whore. One wave of pain followed another for the first thirty seconds of his fuck. Every flick and twist and jab of his joint set off a stronger chain-reaction than the last until my nerve endings were all seared shut with too much of a good thing. Then my brain mercifully took over and convinced my ass that anything this large must be fun. The surges of searing pain transformed themselves to torrents of pure ecstasy washing over my soul. By the time I really felt Eddie's hips pounding into my ass and managed to open my eyes to see what, if anything, was left of my butt, I was having one fine, fucking time. The sight of his massive dick disappearing up my shithole was more of a turn-on even than the feel of his ram-rod stretching me taut. I felt his sweat dripping onto my bare body as he thrusted and pounded away above me. The sound of animal lust in his throat and the smell of his musk surrounding me in a humid cloud of lust added to the feeling I was having the best fucking dream of my life. Now it was my turn to grab handfuls of his chestnut curls and let my fingers slide across his sweaty shoulders and biceps and down across his back. My eyes alternated between his face, twisted in a mask of animal satisfaction, and his dick, drilling harder and deeper into my flesh with every brutal fuckstroke. My ass burned now, but the need to have him shoot off inside my butt was even stronger.

I urged him on, prodding him harder with my heels, calling him a pansy faggot because he couldn't get off, twisting his tits until my fingers hurt. Suddenly I was afraid I'd gone too far. The savage snarl in his breathing died away; he stopped breathing altogether. All he did was quiver and shake and shudder atop me and inside me. His mouth ripped open in soundless rage and then exploded with a stream of Portuguese that sounded like something he wouldn't have said to his own sister. Then I felt his hips drill his dick deeper than ever into my ass, and it was my turn to feel the tide of sailor jism wash through my guts. He pricked and thrusted and fucked and poked up my butt, screaming and tearing at my shoulders with his hands like something out of a bad slasher movie. Watching the adorable agony tormenting his face, I had to laugh — and that made him mad enough to drill me even more. By the time he had pumped his bilges dry, he was pretty much of a fucking wreck himself. After he collapsed into my arms, I let him rest — for about ten seconds. Then I rolled him over onto his back and pulled his legs apart.

He started to give me shit, but I just laughed. I was going to do him again, but first I wanted to suck everything he had. I picked his ass up and carried him into the shower. By the time we were cleaned up, about another hour had passed and we knew each other a lot better. On the way back to bed, I called room service for dinner. By the time it arrived, we'd cum again, too. The rest of that day was even better. The next three built on experience. By the time I limped back aboard to sail away from Rio, I knew for sure that I'd just had the best fucking liberty of my young life.

THE MEAN MARINE

MARK FOX

I'VE ONLY BEEN A PRISON guard a few months, but love the feel. I'm more dangerous than any of these wild, trapped animals in cages. I've got the keys. I've got the control.

This prison is small, close to the Mexican border — a weigh station between the two countries. It's full of brown-skinned killers and drug dealers in for their last time. I got stuck in the lifer wing mostly because I'm a huge fucker and don't take shit from nobody. I pace the walk all day looking over their grimy, tan faces, their bored, hazy, glassy eyes. All of them are faggots looking for a quick jab up their ass. Once in a while, the stupid ones will make a pass at me and I slam their heads against the bars. They kind of grin, then go cower in the back of their cells, watching me leave.

This week, there isn't anyone in the cells. All the lifers being moved to another prison. I got time to relax. I love this kind of job, the power and control over men who've always thought they were tougher than me. Even when a kid, I'd been big and bullying, lifting weights and picking fights with the toughest guys, just to show how bad I was. I joined the Marines when I got kicked out of high school. The discipline did me good and helped straighten me out. But on leave, I was a wild-shit. Me and five other guys would get shit-faced, then go faggot-hunting in the park.

We'd go into the park and I'd walk off alone, my buddies keeping close eyes on who I talked to and where I went. Sure enough, no less than five minutes in the park, some sweet-ass sucker eyes me from his park bench. I go up to him with a cute smile on my lips, swishing my hips a little. I sit next to him and he can't take his eyes off my huge body in uniform. He offers me a cigarette and I take it, thanking him in a real lispy voice as my hand accidentally falls onto his thigh. I feel him tense up, almost ready to shoot his wad right there but he tries to hide it and calmly lights my cigarette with trembling fingers. I take a drag off the cig and settle back, letting my fingers tickle his thigh. Pretty soon his pecker's busting out of his chinos. His throat is all dry. He leans over and whispers his wishes in my ear. I smile and slowly nod my head. He smiles. We get off the bench, walk into the bushes to fuck. I turn him around and rip off his pants, letting the material fall in shreds around his ankles. He's squealing in terror now, because I've also got an arm grip around his waist. I undo my fly, haul out my nine incher, rub it between his ass cheeks, listen to his breath come in gasps. I lean over his back, my mouth close to his ear so he can hear me plain. Then I ram my cock straight up his hole, not caring about his pain or cries, but relishing in the tight clasp of his shitter. I beat my huge prick into him, talking mean to him all the time, my breath beery and hot.

"This is what you wanted, baby. You wanted my cock up you. You asked me to ram your ass with my cock. You love the thought of a big fuckin' Marine creaming your dainty hold, don't you? Nine rock-hard inches bashing your shitter and you love it. You see those Marines and your balls just start jumping, don't they? You just can't let the thought of their huge tits and steaming cocks out of your mind."

I stabbed my hot weapon deeper inside of him as I neared my orgasm. My hands ran up over his bare-skinned belly and half-developed chest, pinching and twisting his erect nipples and then over his hard cock, tugging it a few times, then pulling at his balls. When I start to come, I held his shoulders and thrust up until my balls ground into his and my extra come foamed out into my pubic hair.

I dropped over him, then dragged my damp, deflated cock out. I looked up and all my buddies were there, huge dicks in hand, ready smiles on their faces. I laughed a little and stepped aside letting the next guy in. I loved watching the dainty-assed, red-faced kid when he saw what was in for him next. The look of shock and fear was inspiring and my dick was soon throbbing again. It was great watching those hard, brown cocks pulse outside their starched blue uniforms. None of them took mercy on their victim, but beat his ass like wild dogs. I stood to the side, slowly smoking a cig, watching my buddies wham this lily queer. The sight of these men in blue uniforms coming like wildmen in his ass made me so horny that I needed it again. I hadn't even put my snake away and now it stood out in all its glory, dully glowing from the shit and come. As the last guy was poking his ass, I walked up around to his young face and pulled it up to look in it.

"You're gonna eat your own shit now," I growled and slipped my shaft into his mouth. "You like sucking and eating shit, so suck my cock. Suck me down to my balls." I pushed my weapon in and out of his smooth, rosebud mouth, pressing to the hilt, feeling the cock head graze the back of his throat until he gagged. I dragged it out, only to to slam it in deeper. I pumped his face as a Sergeant jabbed his ass, our rhythm matching; me feeling as though my next haul would crush this boy, bend and break him in half. We came together, the Sergeant's mouth gaping and shouting out wild cries as we released, loud as cavemen, crazed as lunatics, come spurting out of the boy from both holes as we drew away.

Once done, we kicked the punk over and laughed at him. We walked off to piss in the tall grass and get back to base before listed AWOL. We weren't faggots — none of us. We just liked bashing them. It's what they wanted — being worked over by six husky Marines in the park. Once back with the troops, we wouldn't mention what happened but sometimes smile at each other when we saw what the other was thinking.

That was back six months ago. Since then, I've been a guard at Deering and fucking two chicks a week. It isn't unusual for me not to get a really meaningful relationship going with a girl because they're nothing but pussy deep down, anyway. Even when a kid, my best times were with the other guys. We had things in common. Women made me feel good, but they mess up my mind. Guys don't. They're buddies — they're the best.

One of the guys I used to bash fags with was named Lonnie. He and I were closer than anybody anywhere. He lived on base in his own room and was a year older than me. I'd see him every day — practically lived with him. Used to go to his room and lift weights and drink beers. When we were good and shit-faced, we'd cruise the park and bash some sissy-ass. It was better than our girls because a guy's just as strong as you. Lonnie loved it best and took two times, rooting on as I jumped some ass. We'd kick him a couple times and then go back to base to have a few more beers, Lonnie telling me how great it was we were friends and how great it would be if we could live together all the time. I'd laugh and tell him yeah and fall asleep on the floor. He was the closest thing to a brother I ever had and if I loved anybody, it would have been Lonnie.

Lonnie left and moved to California to get a job in the movies. I never saw him again, but everyday I'd check the credits on the television shows to see if his name was there, but it never was. He's been gone nearly three years and I really miss him.

I was sitting alone in my office waiting for the new prisoner. About one o'clock he showed, handcuffed and grimy, a scar over his right eyebrow. The guy was Davis and he was a big fucker, though not as big as me. He was given over to my charge, so I tossed him into one of the cramped little cells. His crime : Murder. The guards left. From here, he was to be taken to another prison and executed.

When I was left alone with him, the rest of the wing was empty of guards and convicts. I stood opposite his cell and watched him like a school kid watches an ape. But my look was a little more sly and a little deeper. He lay on his cot in his ill-fitting blue clothes, staring at the ceiling. He had black hair and a thick, Italian mustache. His face was grimy and the color of rich, dark dirt. He had a broad muscular body, one that had been carefully built up with weights and careful dieting. When he saw I was watching him, he rolled over on his side, shoving his broad back and hard, round ass at me. Luckily, I was bored, so I went back to the office to look up his record. He was my only prisoner. I wanted to know everything about him.

When I read his crime, I nearly cried. It was a strange welling in my chest I couldn't explain, like the reliving of an old pain all over again, only harder. I slammed the file shut and took off for his cell. I stared at him as he slept, his mouth cracked open, his chest heaving slowly. Quietly, I unlocked the metal door and walked in, then slammed the door behind me.

Davis jumped bolt-up at the sound, his eyes wide, scared. I leaned against the bars to give him a moment to wake fully. He raised himself up and dangled his legs over the edge of the cot, a small grin on his face.

"Stand up you scumbag!"

Slowly, Davis stood. I pushed off from the bars and walked to him.

"So you're a killer."

He nodded, no longer smiling.

"Kill a lot of people."

He shook his head.

I grinned now, nasty like. "You're a mean motherfucker, huh? Think you're meaner than me?"

He shrugged, showing nothing in his eyes.

"Drop your clothes, shit maggot!"

He paused, shrugged again and removed his own blue shirt. He had a hairy chest, thick from years of laying muscle on muscle. He took off the rest of his blues deliberately, but not with contempt or hate. He undid his pants slowly, first the top button, then slowly the verticle rows of six, letting them drop in a bundle at his ankles. Then he unsnapped his underwear. They too floated down into the pile. His stomach was flat, his waist trim, a V-angle from his broad shoulders. He was tan all over, but for the belt of white, the perfect outline of a pair of cut-offs. His cock was large and hung heavy from a grove of dense black hairs curling over each other. When he was fully naked, he looked me square in the eye. No challenging. Not humble. Just looking real deep.

I nodded and leered at him, but his face didn't change. I grabbed him by the shoulders and shoved him around so that his large, prominent ass faced me. His globes were covered with coarse black hairs that thickened into a forest in the crack. I smacked one hand on his cheeks and he tensed — but then relaxed. I hauled out my dick, rising in throbs as it engorged with blood. It pulsed in my hand like a live thing. I rubbed its tender, velvety tip across the deep valley of his ass.

"You like that, don't you." My breath quivering the tiny hairs on his throat. "You like guys fucking you ass deep."

"You like it," he said, his voice almost proud.

I paused a moment, then smacked his ear. No one had ever dared say anything to me. I felt myself blushing red. I grabbed his hips and in one forceful thrust, sent my whole cock slamming up his asshole. He winced and cried out but there was no one to hear. After a moment, he was silent, his breath deep and pained,

113

his lips clenched tightly. I stood, my legs spread. My prick ground in even deeper, hoping to kill him with it, to stab him through.

I started pounding him violently, harder than I had ever pounded anyone. Davis thrashed at first, but quickly joined in my rhythm, meeting my pushes with his own. As I creamed his ass, he put one of my hands on his hard left nipple surrounded by a ring of hairs and then put my other hand on his huge, hard shaft. I tried to wrench my hands back, but he held me tight, fistfucking his cock with my hand and rubbing his hard tits with the other. It was only minutes until I came inside him again. I let go of his filthy body and shoved him sprawling on the cot. My anger was hot fire in my throat. I hadn't come in the cell so mad ; the news of his crime was painful, but not as deadly as what I felt. I was crazy mad now. He rolled over and looked in my face, his peter still upright and red.

"You're a motherfucking sonofabitch!" I yelled.

"I know I am," he said lowly. "Is that why you fucked my ass ?"

I hit him hard across the face. Blood started from his lip, but he didn't cry out like I wanted.

"Murdering sonofabitch ! You killed my buddy ! You killed Lonnie !"

Silence. Then : "He tried to kill me."

"The fuck he did ! You faggots are all alike. Out to kill people. Bunch of perverts !"

"Then what are you !" He sat up. "*You* fucked *me* in the ass. You're a faggot, too. !"

I gripped his throat in my fist. "I ain't no faggot !" I said, my face on his.

"Lonnie was," he growled as I clenched his throat tighter. "He was an A-number-one ass-fucker. I killed him because he was crazy and wanted to kill me."

I held him still, but I had to loosen my grip for him to speak.

"You're Bill, right ?" he swallowed and continued, "yeah, you're the one he used to bash faggots in the park with. He was in love with you something wild, man."

I tightened my grip on that. "Lonnie was no faggot !" I howled.

"What the fuck do you mean he wasn't ? He was the best !

114

When you knew him, he was too scared to say so, but when he came out, he came out!''

I couldn't believe this about Lonnie. All my life thinking him the straightest dude to piss on a wall, me thinking him the greatest. It wasn't the same guy.

"He was the same guy," Davis said sadly, knowing my thoughts, his hand resting on my thigh. "And you're Bill. He always said you'd turn out gay. You like bashing ass too much. But what made him crazy will make you crazy. Lonnie loved bashing ass, but couldn't accept being gay."

He was lying under my naked body, his hands free and wandering over me. He had taken control now and I was the prisoner pulling at my prick. Before I knew it, I was ready to come. I looked into his dusty, worn, beautiful face. He opened his mouth and our kiss was tentative, me pulling back at first, scared to venture past the point of hating into the realm of acceptance and love. His tongue slipped in and out of my mouth like a wild darting fish. My hand slid from about his thick throat to behind his head, our bodies pushing closer. In one movement, his head was down, continuing the delicious bobbings of his hand. His tongue was racing over the blue vein now, my back pressed against the hard mattress and cot. He pulled my pants fully off, my eyes now closed and brain swimming in the delight of a beautiful man's touches. Davis rotated my body, without missing a beat on my rock-hard meat, and raised his cock so it swung above my head, brown, thickly veined, a dagger over my face. I stared, then slowly rose to grab the smooth shaft, fingering the balls. Something snapped inside me. I felt dizzy and alive. I ran a hand up through the dense pubic hair to the fur of his slate-flat stomach. I wanted his cock in my mouth. I wanted it, the feel of it, the feel of sucking a man. Pulling on his rod, one hand grasping his rock-hard ass, the cock slowly entered until I encased all of it between my lips. I gagged at first on the heavy, heady smell, but quickened to Davis' pace, wrapping my tongue down the whole, meaty shaft. It was like pure ivory filling my mouth and welling through my whole body. I grasped his ass-cheeks, clenched them and forced his cock into my mouth again and again. My thighs spasmed, his quivered against the sides of my head. Come pounded forth in streams, a river of milk filling my mouth too quick and spilling over my lips. When our balls were dry, I climbed over and lay beside him, our bodies close and warm.

We fucked together for hours, exploring unknown regions of each other's body and soul. He told me about Lonnie and how they met one night in a bar. Mike (Davis' first name) had been picked up by Lonnie, but only because Lonnie wanted to rape and rob him. But back in the apartment, Lonnie's deflowering was easy and they quickly became lovers. Still, Lonnie couldn't rid himself of his feeling of shame and one night got drunk and tried to kill Mike. Mike ended up killing Lonnie out of self-defense, but in court, "a faggot's a faggot and guilty when charged," he told me. Lonnie talked a lot about me and our times in the park, where we bashed the fags. Mike said he was always in love with me, dreaming about me as he rammed the guys in the parks, wishing it was him being pounded as I creamed some punk.

"There was a feeling there, I knew," I whispered to Mike, body on body, "but I just couldn't admit it."

Mike and I kissed and fucked again, tears streaming from my eyes. Above me, I saw Lonnie's face on Mike. The wave of orgasm was never so drenching. I was sleeping with Lonnie's old lover, but also his killer. Yet I understood Mike — I knew how Lonnie could have tried to kill him. I had.

His two days were up quickly and I had to say good-bye to Mike forever, his execution being in three days. The night before he left, I kissed him and thanked him for letting me know myself. He smiled and gently stroked my face.

"Don't let it scare you. It's part of who you are."

I watched him walk down the hall out of my life and I cried. He was not just a man, but someone I felt love for. Being with him made me see that there is no evil in my desires. It had taken me too long to discover this, and it had even killed Lonnie. That's when I swore, as I watched the door close on Mike, that I would be gay and would never be ashamed again, because I was myself.

THE PERFECT PLAYMATE

RICK JACKSON

I 'D NEVER EVEN CONSIDERED answering an ad. I used to read them now and again and wonder about the people who put them in, but that was as far as I went. Then one day I was savoring my latest swingles paper and happened across one that seemed to have me in mind :

NEED RED MEAT

24-year-old California stud in tight shape needs to be taken down a peg. If you are a 20–23 sailor, have bright red hair, a man's body and the will to use it, phone (619) 545–**** and leave a message on the machine.

Area code 619 is San Diego — and 545 is the exchange of Naval Air Station North Island on Coronado. The guy was obviously a marine or another sailor. I fucking *live* on Coronado. Did he know me ? Could the slut have already ogled my ass cruising across on the Coronado ferry ? How many hunky sailors with nine hard, thick inches between their legs could there be in the San Diego area who have rust-colored hair ? What did he mean "taken down a peg" ? As I choked fowl that night and again the next morning my mind kept coming back to the butthole behind the ad. First I just wondered about him. Then I started thinking that calling him up might be fun — not that I'd really meet him — but if I decided to, why the fuck not? I do love marines.

One thing led to another and before I was really sure what the fuck was up, I'd called him and he'd called me and somehow gotten me to give him my address. I knew nothing about the meat other than that he liked sailors like me — but then who wouldn't ? When I opened the door and saw Skeeter, though, I thought this ad business might just work out after all.

He was about 5'10 and looked like a 20-year-old cross between Tom Harmon and Doug Flutie with marine muscles and a bad attitude. I could tell he liked what he saw, too, so I ordered the bastard inside. I'd gotten home just ten minutes before after a long and sweaty day. I hadn't even had time to shuck my uniform. If young Skeeter — and, yes, I told him that was a dumbassed name — wanted to be taken down a peg, I knew just where to start. I planted my ass on the couch and told the kid to pry my boots off and lick my stinking feet. I got more creative later, but just then, that was the grossest thing I could think of. The feel of cool air on my sweaty, aching feet felt just fine. When Skeet's wet tongue slid along the bottom of my foot and worked its way up between my toes, flicking and fluttering its way along my stinking flesh like a podiatrist's wet-dream fantasy, I felt my dick stiffen and knew the kid was just what I needed.

First, I had to make sure we both knew where we stood. I ordered Skeeter to get naked and then take the laces out of my boots while he finished licking the stink off my feet. One lace tied his wrists together behind him. I wrapped the other around his balls and dick, pulling up tight enough to make them hard and purple, but not enough to do any lasting damage. Tugging even more, I moved drill-sergeant close to him and barked, "OK, boot. Here's the story. I'm going to use you for my own private little fucktoy. Since I'm feeling mean just now, I might just damage your pretty little body some. You can beg and whimper and carry on all you want, but it won't change shit. I'm not completely heartless, though. If you're too pussy to take what I have to give, you don't deserve my dick. All you have to do is yell out 'Pussy' to remind me that you are and I'll either let up some or throw your pansy ass out into the hall — depending on how I feel at the time. You got that, boot?" I jerked up hard on the lace and was rewarded with a grunt and whimper by way of reply. My fucking dick was about to explode. I needed relief quick, and, fortunately, I had a flash of inspiration.

Before the bundle of beef knew what else was up, he was hanging from a bar in my bedroom, upside down in an old pair of my gravity boots. I slapped on a new, more comfortable pair and stood in front of him for a few minutes, swinging his face back and forth on my dick. Skeeter may have a weird name, but it suited him one way. As the sucker hung upside down, swaying along my meaty monorail like the side of beef he was, that cute little face of his sucked enough blood up into my stiff crank to make a vampire swoon. He was awkward at first, twitching this

118

way and that along my face-thumping dick ; but when he grabbed hold of my butt to anchor himself, he began sliding up and down my rod like the very cocksucker of creation. Within seconds, his nose was pounding harder and fiercer into my balls while his chin swayed and stroked against my pubes. His lips slid along my crankshaft, coaxing my cream to its doom. His cum-laden ballbag flopped down over his thick, uncut marine dick as he jiggered his face along my joint. Savory though his lizard looked, I wasn't about to suck his wad loose yet — not before I'd broken him in.

Those huge nuts wriggling beneath me like cats in a bag on the way to the river were just too cute to resist, though. The moment my face fell between his thighs, I was lost. My nose sucked in the cloud of man-musk he kept there to lure men to their ruin. I only had room to inhale one nut at a time, but one was enough. I reared my head back like a smug stallion, pulling his tender nuts almost to the breaking point. While I was abusing his ballbag, my hips started meaning business, too. They fucked my dick deeper and harder down his foxy face-hole. The poor bastard wanted to whimper at the way I was using his nuts, but my cock was so far down his throat that all he could do was moan and twist his body around like an electrified bat in the grip of an especially nasty nightmare. I locked my hands behind his head and pounded the living shit out of his face — for about six seconds. Then, the sound of him gagging on my thick dick, the scent of his crotch, the furry texture of his straining ballbag, and the sweaty lash of his cock-sucking lips were too much of a good thing. Some small corner of my brain kept me from chewing his nuts off, but I could tell from the way he gagged on my sweet, thick cream and from the tortured noises he was trying to make that the seizure of satisfaction that wracked my body hurt him a hell of a lot more than it did me.

As I felt my nuts contract and blast everyfuckingthing I had down his tight, hot, marine throat, I lost track of the world for a time. I have a vague sense of our bodies whipping together in the whirlwind of my fuck-frenzy. I have some distant hint of hearing myself yell corny shit straight out of fuck-flicks — crap that I'd never have said if I'd been in my right mind. When I started to come back to the world, though, there wasn't much mistaking the way my hands were tearing at the studly ass hanging just beyond my lips. I'll probably never know whether I rammed my fuck-fingers down his manhole or the bastard took advantage of my momentary lapse in concentration to work his dick-hungry fuck-hole up onto my hand. I know I liked what I felt : the tight, hot warmth of his hole, the surging, yearning power of his guts as they gripped my fingers and pulled me deeper inside him. I also know, though, that by the time I'd run dry, Skeeter's sucker was overloaded and he was letting the remnants of my prime load gush down his face to clot what hair he had. I didn't give a shit about his coiffeur, but if there's one thing no self-respecting sailor can abide, it's seeing good spooge go to waste — especially his own.

I used every ounce of fury my hips and dick had left in them to give his face a couple of last savage strokes by way of punishment, spat out his nuts, stepped back a pace to wrench my meat from off his gullet, and gave him a slap across his jism-smeared face that was brutal enough to send him swinging again. The shocked look on his face was so hot that I suddenly knew what we'd both like. I couldn't resist a long look at his untrimmed meat, leaking pre-cum like an Exxon tanker on the rocks. The sweet, clear ooze had been pounded up against his hard belly and dribbled down in savory rivulets that seemed to slice his pecs into islands of manmeat, just waiting for my teeth to do them justice.

The throbbing in my dick promised an even better time to cum, but first I had to punish Skeeter for sending all those whiptailed little recruits to their futile doom. My hand twitched at the idea of slamming into the hard mounds of marine man-muscle that guarded his fuck-hole, but some whisper of inspiration told me I needed something more. My tennis racket was more. Much more. He heard me rummaging in the closet, but when I turned loose the nylon wrath on his flesh with nothing but a whoosh of air by way of warning, the butch bastard did everything but shit. My forehand tore into his beautiful butt, eating his muscle in an instant of incomprehensible pain. His tender, cream-coloured skin formed mountain ranges separated by red vales of torment. When I tore the butt-biter away from his ass, it looked like nothing so much as a waffle : good enough to eat. I promised myself I'd get around to that, too, before the night was over. First, though, I had to grid his butt until his topography was so surveyed that the only thing left was to sink a shaft.

Each brutal whoosh crashed harder into his butt than the last, sending him arcing out into space like some gorgeous bat, hanging inverted for my pleasure, squeaking through the night, always destined to return for more. His reflexes clenched his muscles tight with every blow and then released to let him moan and groan and beg for mercy. He was sorry. SWAPP. He wouldn't waste any more of my jism. SMACKKK. All he wanted to do was make me happy. THHAAACCKK. When his butt had more lines etched onto it than the motherboard of a 386, I started fucking with him. About every third stroke I'd just let him hear the WHOOSH of doom flying past his butt. His soul would harden for the blow to come and then be disappointed. Then on the next stroke — or the next — I'd slam like doom incarnate into the tender, young flesh covering his marine muscles. At one point, I took a break. The memory of his passion-pointed pecs lured me forward, but I needed somewhere to leave my racket. Then my muse came again. I slathered some hand-lotion along the handle, edged it between his painful buns, and rammed the thick hand-grip about six inches up his butt. I could easily have gone more, but I wanted to make sure my dick would have something tight and fresh to tear into.

His tits were even harder and hotter than I'd expected. I started out like a kindly uncle, letting my wet lips glide up and down his purple passion-stalks while I sucked on him like a babe. My tongue prodded at the base as I turned up the suction. His writhing and moaning got to me, though, so I started to bite down harder, grinding his tit-flesh with my molars until Skeet was half insane with ecstasy. He tried to work his face back to my dick and balls, but I punched his head away. I let him lick at my leg — more because I was too busy to bother putting him in his place than anything else.

Besides, I figured the kid deserved something. As I sucked and chewed, working first on one tit and then the other, licking my way across his hard, hairless chest slimed by sweat and pre-cum, I held his writhing body still with one hand clutched around his nuts and the other on the racket up his butt. His head slammed back and forth between my thighs, delirious with pleasure as I played with him and he twisted slowly in the breeze. After five or ten minutes, though, his tits were tender and my cock demanded action.

I pulled the racket out while I told him how worthless he was, how he couldn't even make a decent faggot, how a man would have been able to keep silent while I was working him over. As I went off on him, I maneuvered my way between his legs. Getting upside down from the bar with inversion boots is a snap — except when you've got another body in the way. Suddenly, though, I was there, sliding naturally between those waffled mounds of muscle. All at once, he was rightside up and we were floating, suspended by lust and desire, our bodies slamming against each other. I breathed in a lungful of his musky scent and felt my racing heart crank up into over-drive. As my dick prodded along the crack in his ass, my lips found one of his ear lobes and pulled at it, slightly at first and then with an insistence born of an ancient hunger. I tongue-fucked his ear and got a cat-like grip on the back of his neck to hold us together — and to let me taste the fear and delight in his skin.

My cock found his shithole on its own ; but once I'd pulled out the racket handle, it didn't take long for him to re-learn shyness. I thought at first how fine ramming my way inside would be. That pre-cum dripping down his chest, just going to waste, made ideal lube, though. I reached around to his cock, forced back his tender cocksock, and put a strangle-hold on his lizard's neck. I slid forward, scraping my dry hand across the super-sensitive tissues of his dickhead, gleaning the harvest of cock-snot he'd been hiding in the secret, most private part of his body. Some monumental surge of will power kept me from loosening my grip on Skeeter's neck to lick my palm clean. Instead, I slathered his load of dick-lube along my cock. I covered Skeet's nose and mouth with my hand so he could smell his scent but couldn't get to it. He opened his mouth to complain and, just then, I slammed my cock into his tight, marine fuckhole with every nasty, selfish, glorious ounce of stud-power I had in me. This time around, I felt his muscles contract — not only around my dickhead, but up and down the length of his studly body. His ass was first to clench tight and then in one ripple of muscle spasms after another that radiated outward, he tensed tight until he just had to breathe. Then he'd open his mouth to gasp for air and I'd fuck him even harder.

I couldn't believe how choice I had it. Fucking in bed or even standing up, you're always bound by gravity. Now, though, gravity worked for us — drawing us back together whenever we sprang apart. Slamming up into his butt was as easy as wriggling in water — I was more swimming my dick up his butt than I was fucking it there. I could sense the pain of his whipped butt and ground hard against the ruins of his ass. His shit-chute was tight and hot and slick. Finding his prostate was no trouble, so I was able to slide my dick brutally across his buttnut on one stroke, and then slam into it head-on on the next. Within seconds, Skeeter just couldn't breathe enough to scream or moan his pleasure. Every twist of my dick up his butt, every lash of my body against his, every grind of my teeth on the back of his neck, every tweak of his tits by my unmerciful hand sent the kid into a tangled jungle of delight that grew darker and more overgrown with every delicious step. The slashing of my machete worked us deeper into the howling, clinging, sweltering undergrowth until we both knew no Stanley could come up to rescue Skeeter's Livingstone. His only hope was that I could fuck him so hard and fast and deep that we could beat our way through the jungle together and emerge at last on the other side.

I felt Skeeter's paws clutching at my ass, urging me onward, but I was lost, far beyond urging. As my body rippled along and inside Skeeter's, as I felt his slick shit-chute sliding across the dry, thirsty skin of my dickhead, as I bit harder into his neck and ass and swagger, I felt myself slipping into the dark void where man must find himself alone. I knew it was inevitable, but the violence of my seizure surprised me. Maybe it was Skeeter's hunky good looks and tight fuckhole. Maybe it was the way fucking upside down made the blood rush to my heads. Maybe I was just in fucking lust. Whatever the cause, I felt my guts turn white-hot and then jet up through my dick, a molten stream of power and lust and perfect satisfaction that blasted off the inside of Skeeter's tight young marine guts and splashed back onto my dick to lube the log for the next stroke. As soon as my lizard got a layer of lube to slide along, I fucked that young manhole harder and faster and more fervently than I'd ever fucked anything, real or fantastic. The sensation of my dick exploding deep inside that hungry fuckhole while our bodies slammed and rippled and swung together was unlike anything I'd ever even dreamed. It was as sweet as fucking in orbit. I discovered later that Skeeter lost his load about the same time I did. At least mine was up his ass; his went to waste again, dribbling down his belly and chest and into his face.

I have no idea how long I used his ass for that first fuck, but it wasn't the record. Those came and went with regularity over the next six or eight months until we settled down. When I lifted Skeeter down and threw his ass onto my bed, I licked the jism and pre-cum and sweat from his body while he panted and squirmed beneath me like the young animal he was. In the months since, we've explored the bounds of lust and love until we're rubbed raw most of the time. That doesn't keep me from raping the fuck out of my cute little marine several times a night, though. After all, marines are tough.

CUMMING OF AGE

RICK JACKSON

I WAS STANDING THE QUARTERDECK WATCH when Dave Putnam reported aboard. He was a seaman recruit just out of boot camp, but he looked so young I thought at first he was some kid who'd gotten hold of his big brother's dress whites to fuck with us. I triple-checked his ID because the kid sure as shit didn't look two months into his eighteenth year. I'm no chicken hawk. I like men with dick and muscle, but Davy was so fresh and innocent, he would make a Zen mystic want to fuck fowl. Once I saw how eager and open he was, I made up my mind to take him under my wing.

I'd seen what the sluts in my berthing could do to boot recruits, and some latent paternal instinct cried out that Davy was special. He was more than just fresh meat for the animals to juice and jettison. The kid was so fucking cute you just naturally wanted to adopt his ass. Fucking it was the last thing on my mind. You might as well talk about nailing the Pieta or the flag or the perfect smell of pine drifting across a mountain lake.

Picture a 5'6" blond kid whose green eyes were wide at the adventure of reporting aboard his first ship. His perfect nose and ready smile set in a strong but beardless jaw were so cute you had to stop yourself from reaching over to tousle his hair. He was the image of the kid brother everybody wants to have, a cross between Dennis the Menace and Beaver Cleaver. The next morning, I happened to be in the head for my pre-breakfast pee while Davy was having a shower. I couldn't help myself. I had to steal a quick glance to satisfy myself the kid had even sprouted short curlies. He not only had blond fuzz, but a mansized piece of untrimmed meat swinging low beneath it. He turned around and showed me a man's firm butt hanging off his hips as he rinsed himself off and made early-morning conversation. Not slack or flabby, that beautiful butt was that rare ass comprising two mounds of perfectly formed man-muscle covered in skin soft and hairless enough to make any tongue twitch. For a moment, it was all I could do to keep from pronging the pleasure out of that soapy hole on the spot. I somehow managed to match his banter and get my dick back into my pants without setting it off, but I knew more than ever that Putnam would take some protecting. That morning at quarters, I sent him on an errand and laid down the law to the rest of the division : Davy was off limits. The guys knew me well enough to know I meant business.

Over the next two months, Davy and I grew closer. The kid was earnest and enthusiastic and impossible not to like. By the time we deployed for our six-month cruise to the Indian Ocean, I was the big brother he'd never had and he meant much more to me than any hole I'd ever reamed. When he let slip one night on watch that he was still a virgin, I promised him I'd set up him.

I had plenty of friends around Subic. The Philippines is to sailors what Switzerland is to bankers. The first time I'd come through, I was still pretending to crave pussy. They did so little for me, though, that I had a rough time getting off. The girls, just thinking I had superhuman stamina, were impressed. Every time I'd gone back since, I went up to drink and visit with the girls and fuck my dick raw with whatever marine ass was in town. The day we tied up, I hauled Davy up to Subic City, poured a couple of beers down his gullet, explained again that in Subic a guy could get anything that came into his nasty little mind, and turned him over to the wildest girl I knew. Melina almost drooled when she saw him; when I told her he was cherry, I could almost hear her panties sop. She grabbed his paw and led him back to make him a man while I, happy I'd managed to keep our relationship all it should be, drowned my lusts in beer and kept an eye open for stray marines.

Looking back, I'm almost sure that once Davy had matured a bit and experienced all the conventional world had to offer, I'd have offered him the unconventional good time. I'm not ashamed of being gay ; gay is good. Gay is fun. It's also more difficult in today's world, though. I guess that's the main reason I was determined to start my little buddy off simple. My mistake was not knowing what a kick in the ass life can be.

Melina and Davy came back after only about thirty minutes. He wasn't grinning like a fool, so I figured something had gone wrong. When I went back to tap a kidney a few minutes later, Melina pulled me aside and said she'd tried everything she knew.

She just couldn't keep it hard — but that if she knew young men the way she thought she did, I'd have more luck. So much for good intentions.

I took Davy out on the bar's balcony away from the jukebox for a talk. We sat on our second-story perch, looking down at the drunks and cars dodging one another in the street below and downed a few more brews while we waited for candor to happen. Eventually, I asked him how it had gone, and he claimed she hadn't appealed to him. I just looked off into the night, but almost at once the barrier he'd kept shut against the world since he'd discovered what his dick was for crumbled before me. The goof began to blather all the fears I'd once felt myself : I wasn't going to respect him any more, he was loathsome and perverted, and all the rest of that dismal, pseudo-moral crap. I suddenly knew two things : he needed a firm lesson in how right sex between men could be — and I was in the best place on the planet to teach him everything he needed to know.

I nearly jerked his ass off his stool. His shorts were around his ankles and his bare, beautiful butt was planted on the balcony railing before he had time to flinch. I slid my hands around to cup that perfect man-sized butt of his — and keep his ass from falling into the street — as I planted my face into his sweaty young crotch. I felt his soft, blond fuzz drifting across my nose and breathed in great lungfuls of the musky scent he'd been brewing between his legs all day. My nose dove down, prying its way between his skinsack and the soft thigh that held it in place. Davy gurgled and sputtered for a moment, but he had a seaman's instinct. His hands found my head and guided me toward the proud manmeat already pounding away against his flat, hairless young belly. My fingers worked his butt cleft apart, sliding along the sweaty, soft secret skin that lived there. His young body shivered excitement in the night air as twin fuckfingers worked their inevitable way closer to his virgin butthole.

Strong muscles pulsed against my fingers as I slicked my hairless way towards glory. I heard some guys shout up shit from the street and knew a crowd had gathered to watch. My mouth was too busy even to smile.

Besides, nothing draws a crowd in Subic like a good show.

Davy had used my face to pry his meat away from his belly. I opened wide and slipped my lips down across the monster dick-head that dominated my world. Even pumped full of lust, Davy's man-meat had enough foreskin left over to nearly cover his best asset. Only the vertical grin of his cum-slit showed through the rumpled crown that hid his hard, pulsing purple meat from the world. A shimmer of pure, sweet pre-cum glinted brightly in the indifferent light and promised me I was doing the right thing. My lips locked hard around his trigger-ridge as my mouth exploded with the first taste of his musk. Part the tangy sweat salt aged to perfection in a young man's crotch, part the lingering memory of some forgotten piss with a slick, steady stream of his luscious pre-cum to flavor his goodness, the relish that raged across my tastebuds was as sublime and perfect and pure as his hard young body as it dangled off the end of his dick. My lips worked even more of his cocksock up his heaving crankshaft until his super-soft 'skin seemed to dissolve into nothingness, floating effort-lessly in the hot, juicy soup that filled my mouth. I felt my spit dribble down between his 'skin and the hot, pulsing prick that waited beneath. My tongue followed, easing gently at first into territory where no one had gone before, scraping its bumpy sur-face across the incredible silken smoothness of his need. Davy was squirming now, moaning loud into the night as I pried deeper and harder, scooping out the stew that had been cooking for eighteen years. Within moments, I felt the salty taste of sweat and musk drowned out by the pre-cum flooding my mouth. As my tongue slithered deeper down into his cocksock, I started sucking like I meant it. My own lizard was so cramped I had to hold on for a moment to step out of my shorts, but young Davy didn't seem to mind the distraction.

Indeed, his hands found their way beneath my t-shirt and slid across the hot, hard flesh of my shoulders and back as he moaned and groaned and cussed like the slut I was teaching him to be. We were both too busy to notice, but in that perfect moment, Davy realized at last what it meant to be a man — and a young sailor on liberty. I felt his man-sized meat take charge and thrust its way up along the length of my tongue. His hands moved to my ears as he fucked his way more fiercely into my mouth. My mouth-organ soon ran out of room even inside his liberal lizard lounge, and his 'skin rippled inside out down across his corona to pile up around his twitching crankshaft. I felt his butt clenching around my hands, working me closer toward his hole. His huge cockhead filled my mouth, and the harder I sucked and tongued, the more the horny bastard wanted and needed. His cherubic mouth was clenched shut in a grimace of unaccustomed pleasure as he fucked my face, deeper and harder and faster with every stroke, slamming my head along his shaft like some out-of-control jerk-off toy. I felt my nose crashing into his soft, blond pubes and his sailor balls hard against my chin. I'd been doing my best to give him the tongue-lashing he deserved, but within moments my mouth wasn't good enough for him. He needed to fuck my throat. I heard his grunts echo off the wall of the bar and mingle with the shouts from the crowd below. Then his hands locked harder around my ears, and my whole world filled with dick as he rammed his way down into the tight, hot tissues of my gullet. If my mouth was too small to do him justice, my throat felt ready to split open.

I tried to suck air on his up-strokes, but I knew Davy was out of control. That beautiful monster dick reamed my throat until I felt my head start to spin from lack of oxygen. I'd wanted the kid to have a good time, but I also needed to suck air. The idea that eighteen years worth of creamy sailor spooge would shoot down my throat as soon as the dam broke was all the more reason for me to make my young buddy happy in a hurry. I felt his body heaving and shuddering, his balls pressing hard against my chin, and his butt flexing and clinching his load up from his spooge-locker. His cannon only needed a trigger to fire, and so I lit his fuse butt good. My fuckfingers had been playing it coy, slipping around his hole and gliding softly over his pucker. Now, I shoved both my fuckfingers hard up his butt and pulled them apart, stretching his ass wide. In my mind's eye, I saw his young sailor butthole grin, but my musings were cut short.

Even with his paws clamped over my ears, I heard the scream roar up from his depths. His cum-tube rippled as one gusher after another of his sweet seaman semen shot straight down my throat. He was too far down for me to taste anything, but I couldn't miss noticing that young Davy was having a very good time. His hard, young body rocked back and forth between spurting his cream filling down my throat and clamping his fuckhole around my fingers. All the while, his hands kept grinding my head down into his crotch. By now desperate for air, I was inhaling his cum with every breath. My ungrateful lungs coughed out his sweet, creamy dick and suddenly, between gasps for his musky, crotch-scented air, I savored his sailor spooge shooting off the back of my mouth, dripping down along my tongue, and setting my soul awash with the glorious taste of his cherry cream. As my lips locked tight around his shaft to keep his load safe, I couldn't help being thankful. He'd waited eighteen years for this night, and I was the hole he'd popped his nut into. From the furious way his hips and butt were grinding and the language he was using, young Dave seemed to be having a good time, too. We kept at it for what seemed a lifetime, but could only have been a few more minutes. I had long since lost track of the globs of gob goo I'd chugged down when his body went suddenly slack. I eased my mouth off his cock, using my lips to really clean his cock for him. I'd learned from other untrimmed meat how tender it is after doing its duty, so I lapped at his lizard until the shouts and shivers made me take pity. I unplugged the man's butt that I'd fingerfucked as a boy's. My mouth found his and I showed him how sweet semen was. He hung helpless in my arms, completely drained by his first face-fuck and too frazzled to think. As I held his naked, young body in my arms, I couldn't help remembering how cute and naive he'd seemed the first time I met him.

The night breeze was drying the sweat on our bodies before I escaped from the spell we had woven together. Even though the crowd on the street below was chanting "FUCK HIM! FUCK HIM! FUCK HIM!" I was surprised when Dave slid his lips against my ear and begged, "Rick, please do me." When I pulled back a bit and asked whether he was sure, he just moaned, "Oh, Jesus, yes."

I pulled his ass off the railing and whirled him around, resting his chest on the two-by-four where he'd become a man. I took a minute to tear off my t-shirt and reached underneath to grab hold of Dave's tits. They were still rigid with lust and, as his butt ground against my hips, begging for everything I had, I mentally cursed the kid for not telling me what he needed straight off. Life is too short not to make the most of every day — and we'd wasted nearly three precious, irrecoverable months. Dave seemed to notice our audience for the first time and showed what a true slut he was. As I put my swollen member against his fuckhole, he yelled back at me that I should do him hard — to show the pussy marines down below how squids could fuck. His shithole told me the truth, though. Dave didn't give a shit about the audience. The way his tender pink hole nipped at my lizard's snout, the way his muscles wrapped themselves around my shaft, and most of all, the wave of gooseflesh that swept across his hard, naked body proved that he needed me for his own pleasure.

Remembering when I first felt a man's massive muscle up my ass, I took my time. My hard dick slid harder and harder against the tender tissues of Dave's fuckhole until, finally, I was through into the tight, slick wonderland of his ass. To give him a chance to enjoy what I had, I stopped dead once my head was inside ; but the young slut wasn't having any. He rammed his butthole up my thick nine inches and wasn't satisfied until the stiff red pubes at the base of my meat were grinding into his shattered ass. The way he was JESUSing and OH FUCKing off into the night showed me his manhole had natural talent. Looking past his writhing body, I saw most of the guys down in the street with their rods out. Some were stroking them off solo, others had mouths shoved down doing the job for them. Something told me, as I felt my hard throb nuzzle into the blind end of Dave's shit-chute, that he would be famous around Subic — for at least a few days until the next young hellhound hit town. I slid my fingernails along Dave's bumpy spine, making him wriggle along my rod in delight. I leaned over slightly so my lips could suck at his ear lobe and neck. He quivered with pleasure as my hot breath jetted into his ear canal, teasing him to crave more. My tongue followed, fucking yet another virgin hole as he squirmed on the base of my cock. His manhole pulsed around my rod, milking my balls like a Santa Monica pro. I began sliding in and out of his slick, hot butt.

Almost immediately, as I felt his shitchute gliding up and over my dickhead, something in the dark recess of my mind clicked off, and I stopped making love to my buddy. As the civilized sailor within me lost the con, my older, more savage self took control of our destiny and ordered all ahead full. I slid my hands around his shoulders and felt my dick slice down into his guts with primitive fury unlike anything I'd ever felt. No longer a shipmate or lover, I was a jungle beast fucking the meat around my dick as though by right of conquest. I felt his hard butt muscles slam against my hips as I humped him faster with every thrust, pounding pleasure up into his ass. His prostate ricocheted off my brutal meat with nearly every cruel penetration of his virtue, sending shivers rippling across his hard sailor flesh. My hips knew what I wanted and what he needed : a solid, bone-crunching fuck. I felt the need : the need to breed. This was about more than simple savage sex, though. Dave was instinctively showing his love and admiration in the most ancient way our species knows : spreading wide and bending over. The single corner of my being that remained rational realized it was no accident I was up his butt. Sure, he craved a thick dick up his butt — but he craved *my* thick dick. As the savage, sensual creature within me took total control, I realized we were now master and slave as much as teacher and student. From our first instant together, this moment had been destined, and I was determined to make the most of it. I stopped trying to guide my dick and turned it loose to ream Dave's tight, squid butt. I pounded upward through his guts, crashing hard up into his tight, quivering hole. My sweaty chest ground against his back as I fucked him. I felt my stiff tits boring into his muscle and soon dug my teeth into his shoulder as I tore into his ass like a jungle cat, hard and fast and brutal. My meat ripped into his guts, but every feral stroke just made him hotter as my backscratcher tore at the itch he was only now discovering. I felt our frenzied fuck-friction fuel his craving as he switched from one OH FUCK after another to a long, low, soul-felt groan of such primitive delight that I knew I couldn't hold out any longer. My balls stopped slamming into his ass and my universe folded in upon itself.

One second I was swept away into the black void which lurks within us all ; the next, my cock and soul exploded into white-hot spurts of limpid light that seared its way out of my dick and up into young Dave's shitchute. I know I pounded on for minutes or hours, because when I finally came back to earth, I was still scrunched over Dave's shoulders, my teeth locked firmly into his shoulder muscle while my dick finished using his butt. My hands, now locked tight around his thighs, held his ass firmly on my dick while my meaty monorail rode him hard. Even after my load had flooded up into his ass, my dick stayed hard. I thought about unpronging his shithole and cranking out another jet of jism into his face ; but sweet and open as that cherubic face was, it couldn't compare to the spooge-slick fuckhole already raping my rod. I turned loose of his shoulder and stood tall, using my hands at his crotch to lift Dave off the ground. He dangled in the air like a rag doll while I used him again, slamming his ass along my thick dick as he howled. I felt his butt crashing into my hips and my spooge leaking out to dribble down onto my balls. Fortunately, I had more cream to ream. Minutes before, I'd fucked myself into a stupor.

This time around, every sensation seemed somehow magnified. Far from falling into a dark fog or fucking along on instinct and autopilot, I played my dick now the way Montana plays his game : hard, fast, and sure. Every scrape of Dave's prostate along my juiced joint, every twitch of his shithole around my crankshaft, every whimper of contentment and moan of pleasure seared its way into my consciousness where it will burn, bright and undiminished until my final hour. My dick and hands at his crotch were supporting Dave just fine, but when I saw him reach out to grab the railing, I lunged forward, fucking him full length against the balcony and bringing fresh cheers from the crowd below. They'd enjoyed seeing his ass before ; now they were able to admire his passion-pumped dick beating against his belly in harmony to the cadence of my fuck-thrusts. From the way he was grunting and groaning and squirming around on my butt-drill, I knew my young fuck-buddy was about to shoot again so I picked up the pace and concentrated my especially nasty work on his prostate. Sure enough, I'd no sooner turned up the heat and sunk my tongue back into his ear when every muscle in his body seized up and he started convulsing. My lizard felt his butt apply a strangle-hold and gave him a second hot protein injection. As my frothy sailor spooge shot up into his butt, the little bastard screamed and twitched and tore around on my tool and did everything but flare up in flames. I might as well had had a high voltage cable up his butt. I was too busy sucking his ear and spunking up his shitchute to pay much attention to the trouble down below, but I discovered later some of the marines got off on having his sailor seed rain down onto them in the street. When I'd finished using his ass for the second time that night, I sank down onto a stool, pulling him down into my lap without bothering to ease my buttplug out of its new home. We were both sweating like the very damned of hell in the tropical heat, but Melina had brought us beers before I could even begin to catch my breath.

When she put her face in Dave's crotch to lap up the spooge that still dribbled from his dick, the little guy squirmed around on my dick like an errant schoolboy. I wrapped an arm around his chest and hugged him tight, telling him to be generous and let her lick the cream from his crop. She deserved it — besides, the evening was young. Within an hour, Dave and I were teaching three marines from the *Barbour County* some manners on the bar's pool table. After that, the beer began to take its toll. I know that when I woke the next morning on the beach, wrapped naked in Dave's arms, we were both very, very messy but very contented young service men.

We dragged our raw dicks back up to the bar to find our clothes, swill a liquid breakfast, and discover who else we'd done. Dave and I spent the rest of that glorious weekend trying to break every taboo the Navy has. We almost made it, too. Most sailors are sorry to leave Subic, but we knew that as the ship sailed off to finish our deployment, my little buddy and I would carry Subic with us forever.

SONS OF PARADISE

RICK JACKSON

I AWOKE TO HEAVEN. My head was still resting on Dalton's thigh, not a foot from his cum-stained log, and Schaffer's meaty arm was lying across my ass. Outside, the trees were full of birds screaming their little lungs out, the surf was making its usual racket, and the sun was well up in the sky : another day in paradise had begun. I was horny even after the action I'd had the night before, but I decided to let Dalt and Schaffer sleep for awhile before starting my day off anew with sex, sun, and surf. As I sat up and watched them sleep, I thought back over how we'd come together. My idea had happened at Subic Bay. Most sailors love the Philippines, of course — a girl, a room, and all the beer you can drink can be had for $10. For those who prefer dick, the place has all the fascination of any other third-world port : beggars, orphans, rotting ruins, sleaze, and disease. Trying to make the most of my liberty, I headed for *The Toast* — the gayest nightspot in town. I think most sailors have a subconscious craving for marine ass — and the *Barbour County* had docked that morning with two hundred of the sex-starved, hard-muscled, tight-assed jarheads. I was sure some of them would be at *The Toast*.

What was a surprise was to see RM2 Dalton there because I'd lusted after him since he came aboard. He spends most of his time in the weightroom pumping every muscle to perfection or in the head showing them off. Sailors aboard ships often run around heads starkers, but this guy was something chronic. He'd pick the shower directly in front of the pissers and then keep the curtain open, spending ages massaging soap across his enormous tanned, hairless chest and down into his crotch. His rod goes on forever and he never neglected to trap his cock against his leg and soap the shit out of it. Then he'd rinse off and move out in front of the mirrors to towel himself dry. Sometimes he spent so much time admiring himself that a simple shower took him 30 minutes. Even outside the head, his favourite subject was his

"Kaaaaaaaaaaaak." He'd work every subject around to his "Kaaaaaaaaaaaak" and then pronounce the word like a cantor praising his boss. The minute I saw Andy Dalton on the dance floor, I knew he was mine. I'd have my eight hard inches unloading sailor spunk into that gorgeous ass before the night was out. Then I had my thought : why just that night ? Since we military types are all tested shitless for HIV, drugs, and everything else but bad breath, it occurred to me that by sticking to service dick, I'd have all the beautifully creamy, pearly-white, totally pure spunk I could swallow. Why stop with one dick when we could put together a dozen ? We could fuck and suck in the kind of absolute party freedom unknown since this AIDS disaster began. If Boccaccio could use the *Decameron* ploy to escape the plague before Reagan was born, why wouldn't it work now ? I was already planning to get an apartment when we got back to Pearl so I'd have a place to get away from the ship. I'd need a roommate ; why not a dozen hunky USMC pure roommates ? If several of us got together, we could afford a house ! By sticking to squids and jarheads who lived there, we'd not only be able to fuck in comfort but we'd already have prime beef on hand — beef we were *sure* wasn't infected.

I was so excited by my idea that I forget my plan to stick my Kaaaaaaaak down Dalton's throat. I stroked right over to him and dragged him, open-mouthed, into the corner for a chat. After I blew off the "What are *you* doing here" shit, he began to concentrate on my proposal. He was all for it and even suggested we include another Adonis, an OS3 named Schaffer in the group ! Business done, we headed for the back room. I pulled his pants down and went right to work on his fuckhole. His cheeks were even more muscular than they seemed ; working my tongue all the way to his hole was a real job — but one worth the effort. Long before I got there, my head was swimming with the scent of manmusk. My tongue slid smoothly along his hairless crack until it finally reached its goal, hidden deep and dark, secret from the world. As I manhandled his Kaaaaaaaaaak, I lapped and slathered, prodded and poked, and grooved on his ass until my tongue was so tired it was about to fall off.

He moved away to strip off his clothes, but I wasn't having any of that. I wanted him with his pants around his knees like some trashy stud in a darkened theatre. His ass was wet; my cock was stiff; the time was right. I pulled his shirt-tail toward me and I rammed my ass-starved cock into his tight squid ass. He yelled in pain as I crashed through into his ass because of the size of my own cock, but I wasn't about to let him escape. As I pounded into him like a pile-driver on speed, driving him slowly across the floor on his knees, I told him that if he was so proud of his own tool, he shouldn't begrudge me mine. I fucked him with a pent-up lust and rage I hadn't known I had. My months of desire escaped into him through my cock; my rage at being kept in the dark about what he really wanted erupted deep inside his guts as I splashed my way into him. Still unsatisfied, I kept at it, slowing briefly to catch my breath and then building for one more massive protein injection. The damage I was doing his prostate caused him to shoot off about the same time I refilled his shit-chute. I reached up to wipe my dick with his shirt-tail and collapsed onto him, letting my tongue explore his mouth as it had his ass. After an hour or so, we moved to a hotel for the rest of the weekend, knowing that it was to be only the first of many.

A week after we'd hit Hawaii, we found our Xanadu, just twenty minutes west of Pearl. Set on an isolated cove, surrounded by bush, the house has a spotless, wide sandy beach just made for love in the sun. Dalt, Schaffer, and I each knew of a couple other hunks we thought might be interested and, within a week of finding the joint, we'd signed the papers and moved in.

Our "house rules" were simple :

a. Only folks (military or civilian) with a year's clear record of ELISA testing can join us. Guests and pledges who haven't been "clean" for nine months can frolic, but in such cases kissing and sucking or fucking without rubbers is *verboten*!

b. Anybody stupid enough to mess with folks outside the group is bounced out on his slutty ass.

c. Monogamy isn't exactly discouraged, but we all think practicing it is dumb in a house filled with meat like this. Folks sleep wherever they want.

Most of us have lived here since the beginning, two years ago now. Folks sometimes leave for several months on deployment and we sailors have to stay aboard on duty days, but there's always enough dick to go around.

Schaffer rolled over and brought me back to the present, which was just as well. I was ready for action again. I'd come back the day before from six weeks of EASTPAC, and we'd celebrated most of the night; but I was still far from being spunked out. From the time Dalt had introduced me to Mike Schaffer, I'd been in lust. They had met at the Pearl gym where they worked out when in port. Schaffer (whom I call Slick because of his nearly hairless body) is even better built than Dalt. He has clear, deep blue eyes, a perfect pug nose, about six dozen perfect teeth, and tightly-curled, thick blond hair in the appropriate places and none else besides. His arms, legs and neck are nice, but his chest and belly are what turn me on. Both his nipples swell like nothing human, standing rosy and hard above his enormous, bulging pecs. Even asleep, his belly rippled with muscles down to the groin. His cock isn't especially long — I'd guess about seven inches, average for our house — but it's the thickest I've ever seen. The amazing thing is that it's the same width all the time. Erect, it pushes out from his golden curls to reach its full lengh; but even limp, the monster is well over two inches across. I'd tried several times to take it up the ass, but haven't managed it yet. The night before, I'd tried again but, in the end, I'd had to settle for Dalt's tremendously long but rather narrower prong up my passion-starved ass while I made use of Slick's tight, hairless hole to hold all I had stored up during the month and a half at sea.

As Schaffer stirred, I saw his blue vein throb encouragement. I leaned over and began to use my tongue on him, reaching under his bare ballbag to get at the remains of the last night's fuck. Once I'd cleaned him up, I inhaled his balls one at a time and lovingly massaged them with my mouth and tongue. It was easy to see that Schaffer still had more loads to deliver. Not only were his balls still packed with prime stuff, but his cock again demanded attention. I released my grip on his ballbag and moved up to take as much of him into my mouth as I could. The pre-cum already glistened in a stream trickling down from his piss-slit toward his muscle-knotted belly. I used my tongue to advantage, giving broad laps across the head to capture every trace of the pre-cum before I moved on to the job of getting him into my mouth.

Not surprisingly, our games had awakened Dalton, who, always greedy for manjuice, insisted on joining in. By the time I'd gotten Slick into my mouth, Dalt had his tongue up my ass, one hand on my nuts, and the other going hell-for-leather at my rod. Schaffer's dick is difficult enough to suck when you can give all your attention to working the thing around without snagging it on the odd tooth or triggering a gagging reflex, but when you're being buggered by the fastest tongue in the west and jerked off by the long arm of the fleet, you just have to say, "Fuck it."

"Fuck it," I said to them as I dislodged the sailors' parts from my body. "I don't know why I'm working so hard, anyway. Except for last night, you two no-load squids haven't had to do shit for six weeks; you can fucking well make up for it now." I stretched out between them, put my hands behind my head, and told them to get the fucking evolution underway.

Dalton rose to the challenge and bestrode me, squatting down impaling himself with a grunt, a moan, and a shit-eating smile upon my pride and joy. As I lay beneath him, watching his thick, muscular legs raise and lowering him along my shaft, I got off as much on the spectacle as I did the job his tight ass was doing to my tool. I haven't told you much about Dalt's body yet, mainly because I'm afraid I can't do it justice. The dude is unbelievable. I've lived with the guy for two years, and I still catch my jaw hanging open now and then in awe of his beauty. He's built along the same general lines as Schaffer — the heavily-muscled weightlifter type. His chestnut hair is thick, and his awesome jaw contrasts with his cute little nose. The major focus of his face, however, is his eyes. Long light-brown lashes surround ethereal deep green eyes that would make Michaelangelo's *David* come bucketsfull. The eyes don't look at you — they radiate. When Dalt looks at you, you're captivated by the sparkle. I've seen girls follow him on the street trying to think of some way to get hold of his dick, they love his eyes so much.

You shouldn't infer from all this eye-talk that there's anything wrong with the rest of him. On the contrary, he's juicy all over. He has a smile that would stop a tiger in his tracks. His thickly-muscled neck gives way to broad, tanned shoulders, and beautiful weightlifter's arms ; his pecs and gut are perfect. Like Slick's, his body is nearly hairless ; but Dalt has fine hairs sticking out of the edge of his tits and a small ridge of fur runs down form his navel to his "Kaaaaaaaaaak." Twin clumps of light brown muscle comprise his ass — two perfect handfulls which carry the theme of his surfer's tan into a rhapsody. Between the clumps, we lucky few know where to find the hairless pink pucker which guards a chute with muscle control unlike any in Christendom.

You can imagine how it felt lying there to have this creature sliding up and down my pole, caressing it, using wave after wave of upward muscle contractions to urge my load up into his depths. Even without Slick's nipping at my tits, I'd have been hard-pressed to hold off for long. When Slick moved behind Dalt to begin licking my ballbag and Dalt's ass, I tried to slow down by concentrating on wrapping my hands around the "Kaaaaaaaaaak" to give it the handjob of the century ; but instead I lost all control and felt my hips take on a life of their own, thrusting shot after shot up into Dalton's tight, hot pleasure tunnel.

When I'd finished, I ordered Dalton to his knees so that Slick could ravage his hole. Slick was all for getting into it, and he was able to fit The Monster into Dalt's ass since my rod had pried wide the gates. As Slick rode his ass, I stuck my slime-covered dick as far down Dalton's throat as our position would allow. Slick and I exchanged deep kisses while my hands worked at Dalton's tits and Slick's ass in about equal measure. Slick's hands were kept busy finishing the world-class handjob on Dalton that I'd been unable to administer. We all came at more or less the same time — Slick ramming his thick rod into Dalton's savaged hole, slamming his pubic bone against Dalt's tight ass with each stroke. When I saw the eyes roll back in Slick's head and knew what was happening, I lost it again — this time down Dalt's throat. Just as he finished sucking dry the last of my load, I felt Dalt shudder as Slick's hands and the pressure on his prostate forced Dalton to gush out his pearly manhood in shot after shot, covering the bed, my legs, and himself in sticky glory.

By this time, it was about 10 A.M. Four of our jarheads with more hair around their dicks than on their heads walked past the door of our fuckroom on their way to a morning's sunning on the beach. One of them — a rimming specialist by the name of Fritz Muller whom we all called Oscar because of the size of his sausage — popped his head into the room and said, "Are you sluts still at it? Forchrissake, you'll go blind for sure! Why don't you give it a rest — or at least move it outside to catch some rays. Besides, I feel like a taste myself." Never a bunch to look an asslick in the mouth, we went along. The day was early enough for the sun to be cool as we moved outside to our beach to collapse into another fuckpile. As I felt tongues at my cock and ass and an uncut cock at my mouth, I knew that life for us would continue to be Paradise.

JARHEAD LOVE

RICK JACKSON

I'D BEEN STATIONED at Subic for a year, so I knew all about the head at the Spanish Gate. It's hard for officers to cruise crappers without being obvious, though, so I generally found love at the pool or the gym. Besides, you generally find more foxy, naked flesh there than sitting shit-assed on the crapper. Still, when I stopped by the head to take a serious dump, I kept my eyes open. When the screw holes in the partition darkened and I felt his eyes on me, I let him look. Why not? I was 24 and built like a god. Shit, I admit it. I didn't mind giving the poor guy a thrill. I even stuck around after my business was done to check him out. I wasn't cruising. On the other hand, when I put my eyes to the hole and saw his hand sliding up and down his monster shaft, it didn't take me long to appreciate a good thing. That massive marine manmeat would have been hard to miss. He was about two inches longer than me and just as wide. Size can be nice, but the perfection of that lizard was even more a turn-on. Something about it practically glowed youthful studliness. His hand was doing some serious pumping up and down his kid-skinned crankshaft, but he stopped short of gliding up across his head. His fist almost shouted out that the shaft was all it could handle — that something else would have to take care of the head.

I was concentrating so much on his handiwork that I failed to notice the drop of pre-cum forming in the corner of that lizard's eye. When he stopped going after it for a moment, I figured something was up and scrunched down to get a view of the top half of his cock. By the time I caught the light sparkling back at me through that tasty droplet, the buttwipe was nearly on top of his pre-cum jewel. The gods gave me a single glance and then it was gone, soaked up by a wad of toilet paper. Pre-cum has always turned me on big-time. For some reason I can't understand, I never juice up. No matter how pumped my 'nads are, I don't ooze shit until the top of my head blows off and there's naval cream everywhere. Just looking at the way he dabbed at the thick, translucent dicklube made my tongue twitch. I yearned to ease into it and then pull away to watch the drop become a long, shimmering thread of man-sugar. He obviously thought of his blessing as a bother. Once his cock was cleaned, he adjusted his ass on the seat and went back to work. Yeah, I know you're thinking you would probably have buttoned up and left the guy alone to his fun. And the check is in the mail, too.

When I finally managed to frame his face in my tiny peephole, I nearly fell off the crapper. Most crapper-cruisers are distinctly used goods. This dude was no geezer wtih a massive pot belly and no dick. He was the best looking piece of marine beef on the hoof I'd seen in weeks — and believe me, around Subic you see plenty of marines good enough to eat. At first I couldn't believe I'd missed seeing him around the gym. Then I remembered that the *Tuscaloosa* with three times a hundred sex-starved young troopies had sailed in the morning before. About 19, the kid had the cropped hair and seriously grim expression that left little doubt that he was one of the few good men the Corps had built. They had a lot to work with in his case, though. His bone structure looked something of a cross between Tom Cruise and a young Richard Gere, except that his eyes were a radiant blue. His tongue hung absent-mindedly out of the corner of his mouth as he fucked his fist and made him look even younger — and cute as a bug's ear, besides. I saw his eyes flick from the business in hand up to my peephole. Assured I was watching, he picked up the pace even more until I was afraid he'd pleasure himself to a blister. I slid down to admire his other bone structure and decided it was time to put all those Academy courses in leadership to some useful purpose. I won't bother sketching out the next several minutes. We did the usual pick-up shit, writing on buttwipe and passing it under our partition. When he discovered I had a single room at the PCS BOQ, he wrote back he'd be over before I could get my pants off.

He almost made it. I dragged him over to the bed as I put a beer into his paw on the way so he'd have something to suck on, too. He didn't get to the beer for hours.

Even before I unzipped his gear, I was surprised at his size. He stood only 5'8'' off the deck, but the bulge in his shorts was Boston Celtic material. When his meat popped free and slapped me in the face, I knew I had a very long evening before me. I started to take my time, breathing in great lungfuls of his delicious crotch as I nuzzled his balls with my nose and massaged his nuts with my tongue. They hung low and heavy between strong thighs, promising to deliver everything I could ask for. I'd no sooner started in before I sensed my beautiful young jarhead was trying to have a thought. His hands on my ears pulled me upward until I stood before him and he was caressing my pecs and circling my hard nipples withh his fingers. Then I remembered the key to dealing with marines.

I've never figured out whether marines come into the Corps with inferiority complexes or boot camp just convinces them they're piles of shit. I've never met a marine yet, though, that deep down didn't feel he was so worthless that he didn't deserve pleasure. I think that's why they all get off on giving pleasure to others — and especially being fucked up the butt by US Navy dicks. The fact I was an officer was probably a special rush for him. I suppose there must be marines somewhere that aren't major turn-ons who underestimate their worth, but I've never found one. My little blue-eyed, big-dicked Gomer lifted my shirt off and began sucking at my bare tits, easing his boyish lips across my raging nipples on a thin cushion of spit. Those lips and tongue might as well have been hooked directly to Hoover Dam. Jolt after soul-shattering jolt ricocheted through me until I had to pry his face away for my own survival. I like getting off as much as the next guy, but the evening was too young for me to cream my jeans. Just to make sure that didn't happen, I finished getting naked — and pushed him down onto the bed for some serious cocksucking.

He seemed upset when I slithered between his legs and sucked one cum-clogged nut into my mouth at a time, but I wasn't about to juice this stud and let him mope off into the night. The smell of sweat and musk enfolded me in a cloud of bliss that seemed to hold us both suspended. I felt his heels dig into the small of my back and his hands begin to work their way carelessly through my hair. My hunger for his huge flawless dick drove me north, lapping the bottom of that throbbing piece like any other hound with an especially meaty bone.

By the time I was eye to eye with his lizard, he'd oozed a pool of pre-cum down onto his flat, bare marine belly. A slender thread of the sweet goo hung from his throbbing cock like a stalactite. I started on the source, sliding my tongue under his cock and scraping him marine clean. When my tongue couldn't reach any more down his cum-slit, I ignored his massive manly member and attacked his belly with my lips and tongue. As I kissed and slithered and slurped around and into his belly-button, sucking up every delicious drop of his dick-lube, his body shuddered and arched as his legs wrapped even harder around my body. I suddenly realized neither of us had said a word when he started to moan and swear quietly to himself. The harder my tongue probed his navel, the louder he got — but I didn't give a shit just then if COMNAVSURFPAC himself heard us going at it. My only concern was that I was running out of goody. It was time for me to do some serious cock-sucking.

The kid was so big, though, that I had trouble. I'm a 4.0 cock-sucker, so when I couldn't get much of him into my slutty mouth, you know he's big. I satisfied myself at first by sliding my lips across his huge pulsing dickhead, sucking enough to let him know I meant business while my hands kneaded his balls and teased his tight little butthole. The more I worked at getting him into my mouth, the bigger the dick swelled. I sucked from the bottom at one lobe at a time and took periodic time outs to feed on the dick-drool he constantly oozed. His groans and the randy thrusting of his hips left little doubt he was having a good time, but I needed him inside me just then more than I'd ever needed anything in my life.

Shifting around into a better sixty-nine position, I managed to work his head into my yawning facehole. I was just starting to do some justice to his meat with my tongue when he lifted my hips and dropped me onto his face, slamming my cock down his throat. The bastard was even better at sucking dick than I was. He took all eight inches down his tight jarhead throat like a sword-swallower with an iron deficiency. Before I could even get my tongue behind his trigger-ridge, that greedy cocksucker had his lips nuzzling my stiff red pubes while the super-tender tissues of his throat did things to my head I'd never even dreamed possible. Every pulse of my heart echoed through my dick and was countered by gripping, massaging muscle inside the jarhead's high-suction gullet. His tongue slid along my crankshaft like butter across corn until I knew I had to escape from his grip or blow my chances for slow sex right along with the best nut of my young life. As I worked myself farther and tighter along his throbbing shaft, I reached down with a hand to pry his face off my crotch. It was work ; the bastard wanted to stay put. Finally I was able to lift myself high enough on my knees that he had no choice but to drop off. As soon as I felt his head hit the pillow, I plopped down hard, trapping my meat against his bare pecs, and put my cocksucker into overdrive.

Nothing kept him from going after my balls and ass. I could take the ball-handling, but when he moved up and began tonguing my butthole, I thought I would fucking die. He didn't prod right in the way most young grunts do. He took his time, sliding his tongue up along my buttcrack, flicking his way around my hole until every nerve begged for relief. Then, when he'd teased me just a moment too long, he'd dive into my shitchute with his long mouth organ, prodding here, caressing there, until I knew what heaven felt like. His fingers held my butt against his face as he raped my willing ass. All I could do was try to ignore the exquisite torment of his tongue and work on his man-shaft. I sucked and tongued that marine meat with my mouth while my throat held his business end in its loving, velvet grip. My hands slid down to massage his own butthole and play with the hard mounds of manmuscle that guarded the entrance to his soul, but I was too far gone to do quality work. A stone statue would have melted under the torture of that troopie tongue ; I was anything but stone. Time began to slow from minutes to slurps and from seconds to dick strokes as we ground and sucked and tongued at each other just the way America's fighting finest should.

After time blurred and I lost track of the world, I have no clue how long we rocked together, building need to lust and thence toward the explosion violent enough to shatter our cosmos. After seconds or hours of bliss, I felt my ballbag tighten despite myself and, somehow, managed to hold off. I flew up and away from his greedy mouth and moved back between his legs. This time, as he lay on his back with his legs raised, I went at his ass with my tongue. He was the first man I'd ever felt the desire to rim, but when I found the tight rings of muscle that was his fuckhole, nothing would have held me back. I slid along his hairless ass-crack, expecting to be grossed out any second, but found only manmusk worthy of the very gods. By the time I felt myself prodding face-first into his butthole like the slut of creation, I had long since lost my priggish prejudice and wanted only to work myself up into his guts. The kid wriggled his ass against my face and filled the room with moans and groans and grunts of delight. Driven by the delicious wickedness of rimming almost as much as I was lured by his tight marine butthole, I kept tongue-fucking his ass until he leaped away from me.

I must have looked as though my dog had just died. He lay heaving for a moment on the bed and, sticking his butt in my face, went to his elbows and knees. I lapped at his dangling balls for a moment and then went back to his butt with my tongue. With his ass in the air, I was able to work even farther in. I pried and probed new delight with every lash of my tongue, but it wasn't enough for my horny young grunt. He craved something meatier up his jarhead ass. When he finally spoke to me, I was startled at first. Ever the gracious host, though, I was willing to give him what he was begging for : "Please . . . Fuck me!

You can't ask for it clearer than that. I was already in such a fuck-frenzy that I forgot all about lube. Fortunately, my tongue must have gotten him ready, because when I put my lizard on station and lay my chest across his strong back, the kid didn't mess around. Even before I could ease my eight inches of naval weaponry down into his marine spooge magazine, he arched his butt back and pronged himself onto me. I head a gasp and then a long, soulful "Yeeeesssssssssss" as I knelt quietly, draped across his back, for a few moments. My hands explored what my tongue had missed : the hard points of his tits and the steel muscles that lay below them, the broad jarhead shoulders, and his sleek, thoroughbred flanks. I pressed his dog tags against the flesh of his chest and sucked at the chain as it met his neck. My lips moved up to suck at his ear lobe. I felt him shudder as my breath came in short, feral blasts against his ear. One hand slid across the close-cropped marine cut to find the Bambi-soft hair that crowned his head. Suddenly unable to wait for love, I slipped into a whirlpool of lust.

My fist gripped his hair, I locked my teeth into his muscular shoulder, and my lizard began to eat his ass for dinner. Each slap of my pelvis against his hard marine butt sent a fleshy shockwave of thwack echoing off the walls of my room. Every time my hard-headed cock slammed into the blind end of his shit-chute, he let a short, careless grunt escape his clenched lips. As my cock reamed his foxy hole, the muscles of his guts rippled along my crankshaft like the fingers of a velvet glove, drawing my zero spooge closer to glory. I was shocked at my own brutality, but he expected nothing less. His marine soul craved brutal domination. My hands tore at his pecs, pulling me tighter and harder against his sweaty back as my hips flew in and out, untainted by any mercy. My cock found his prostate and used it as the anvil of my lust. The slap of my balls against his and the rasping of my breath into his ear and the silken feel of our bodies sliding willy-nilly together overloaded my consciousness until I was left with a bliss-ful blur, one sensation coasting into the next delight and then into eventual ecstasy. Only one fragment of my brain functioned and it heeded the most ancient call of man : fuck it hard, fuck it deep, fuck it again.

I have no memory of sinking into the black fugue that claimed me. I can only guess how long we pounded and slammed and slid together on my monorail of boneflesh, riding together to-wards the communion of our kind. I know only that my universe exploded suddenly into a furious delight unlike anything im-aginable. Every nerve in my body must have blazed at once as my squid spooge blasted up from my bilges and flushed down into the tight, dark refuge of his tight marine butt. I do know that I came back to the world to find myself humping his hole like a mongrel cur fucking a stray bitch in the street. My paws were locked onto his sweat-slicked young body and someone was screaming and swearing like a bo'sun with his nuts in a vise. As my body flailed helplessly into his, I discovered the screams were my own. Young studly was screaming, too, but his screams were the non-verbal, inarticulate noise of complete satisfaction. My hands found his thighs and, as I let his shoulder escape the grip of my teeth, I locked us together ass and dick until every drop of my US Navy ballast was pumped far enough down his hole that he'd need a week to shit it out.

When, at last, I found myself dry-humping his hungry marine butt, I gave one last gurgle and collapsed onto his body, a heaving, sweating wreck. He wasn't in much better shape. We lay a tangled mass of satisfied flesh until I felt our sweat begin to dry. My marine eased his hole off my cock and was on his feet before I focused on what was going on. The idiot figured since I'd gotten mine, the evening was over. His regulation marine inferiority complex made him reason that no one — and certainly not a sexy and very satisfied stud like me — would want to mess with him once I'd gotten my nut. He gave me a silent, sappy grin as he started to work his stiff dick back into his shorts. Unable to do more than shake my head at jarheads in general and him in particular, I got up, grabbed his paw, and pulled the magnificent bastard into the shower for a long, slow, steamy fresh-water washdown. When we'd finished, I almost had to drag him back to my bed and up my butt. His cock nearly broke my ass open, but once he was inside, I never wanted him to leave. I'm sure you're not interested in the lurid details of what we did with the next eight hours. Let's just say that by the time he hauled his ass out of my BOQ at reveille and I dragged my raw dick down to PSO for officers' call, we'd set new records in inter-service relations. About noon, I heard that the *Tuscaloosa* had pulled out. Looking back, I know the night I spent with that sappy, insecure young marine stud was one of the highlights of my life. That makes it all the stranger that the only words either of us spoke to the other were his "Please . . . Fuck me."

HARD ASTERN

RICK JACKSON

W HEN YOU SLEEP WITH sixty other guys in a destroyer's
berthing compartment, you notice dicks. Even in our
home port, the supposedly straight guys are always ragging each
other about their dicks. You can bet that I spent plenty of time
thinking about cockmeat on my six-month deployment through
the Indian Ocean. While most guys aboard are dreaming of all the
wet pussy waiting for them in Asian fleshpots, my waking and
sleeping dreams were crowded with all the huge meaty cocks I'd
seen swinging loose through the compartment. I'm not unique ;
every gay sailor knows what I mean. The pressure builds every
time you see one of those jock joints gliding past your rack on the
way from the shower. You look across at night and see the dick
sleeping opposite you standing tall above cum-choked balls and
know how sweet it would be to wrap your lips around his
problem and help a buddy out. As the days become weeks, you
know you'll fucking explode unless you find something tight and
warm to slide your craving cock into.

My first deployment was only a decade ago but it seems
another lifetime. Times were different back then : once ashore,
you could fuck and suck until you had pumped out everything
you had. You knew the worst you'd come down with were raw
meat and a case of the clap. We were two days away from my first
Asian fleshpot when the Iranians took over the embassy. The first
we heard about it, of course, was when the CO came over the
horn and said that our port visits were cancelled. We were bound
for the Gulf. We didn't know it then, but we'd stay there, floating in the sweltering heat for seven, long, thick, throbbing
months. Fortunately for me, Bob was even harder up than I was.

Oddly enough, Bob Shepherd had the one dick in berthing that
never came up in my fantasies. In fact, we'd always given him
shit about how small it was. Something about his boy-next-door
good looks made everybody like him, but he was the kid-brother
type rather than a Mr. America. Back then, I didn't need a
brother, I needed a tight fucking hole to ream. We'd been in the

Gulf for about three weeks and had had GQ's every day. The CO figured the US wouldn't put up with its embassy being captured and would want us to kick Shi'ite butt. He was going to be ready if it killed us. When the GQ Klazon went off at 0330, I knew we were in for another cluster-fuck until reveille. I groaned and shoved my hard, thick eight inches into my dungarees as I headed for my battle station thinking dark thoughts about life in the Navy.

Shepherd showed up about ninety seconds later, we dogged down the watertight hatch, and were sealed in with our gear for the duration. The worst part about GQ's for us was staying awake, because unless they really started shooting missiles off, we didn't do shit. They cut the ventilation first thing, so it got hotter than a sand-hog's crotch. About five minutes into GQ, they secured the power and the only light we had was from a single battle lantern. We'd been locked in the sweating in the dim for about twenty minutes when I fist noticed Bob was acting spooky. He had been in the Navy for five years, so he wasn't nervous or claustrophobic or anything. I assumed he was either on something or the heat was getting to him. We'd both long since pulled off our shirts but were sweating like pretty boys in a Turkish prison. He had a twitchy sort of look about him and sounded as though he were stuck in fast-forward. When I told him to shut the fuck up, the guy turned about nine shades of crimson and apologized. Then he started in on how horny he was — as if I gave a fuck. He droned on about how his balls hurt so he jacked off and the more he shot, the more his 'nads pumped out. I told him my dick hadn't been soft since San Diego so I wasn't interested. If he couldn't score a good time off his hand, he should find a faggot to suck him off. That idea woke the poor bastard up quick enough. Did I know of one ? He'd pay $200 cash for a blow-job.

You can probably imagine I was starting to pay more attention to Bob's problem. I thought for a minute and said I didn't know anyone who'd do it for money, but I might know somebody who might be willing to *trade* blow jobs. I could just make out the hard head of his uncut cock peeking out of his dungarees. It was pressed against his sweaty belly and made my own good news throb extra-hard. Bob torqued out big time. He wasn't a fucking

151

faggot. He'd rot in hell — as though we weren't already — before he'd suck dick. I smiled and changed the subject. About five minutes later, though, I brought it back to how I was ready for liberty and some prime-assed bitches to hump. I rambled on with stories I'd heard guys tell of Thailand and the Philippines, putting myself in the saddle until my poor lust-struck buddy didn't know whether to jism his jeans or crap in them. Finally he gave in and asked me who I'd heard about. I played it coy and told him that I'd *heard* a guy would suck dick as long as he got his lizard licked first — that he wasn't about to clean some dude's cock and then get shafted, so to speak.

Shepherd was hooked. He'd do anything, as long as he got off into something other than his hand. I undid the first couple of buttons on my dungarees, my dick did the rest. When I was standing tall, I just said, "OK, here's your turn at bat. Suck on this, sailor boy." He started to pussy out : he couldn't do it at GQ, he had to work up to it, and a pile of other crap. I told him to suit himself, but once I put away my gear, he could work his bone to a finger for all I cared — it was pretty much finger-sized to begin with. He looked in the uncertain light at my pulsing, purple one-eyed monster glistening with the sweat pouring from my chest. I saw his tongue snake out across his lips as he measured his need against the humiliation of having me know he was a cocksucker. He was partly right : even as he was deciding to wrap his Luke Skywalker-style face around my cock, I knew I'd give him a hard time. Everybody in the Navy calls buddies "Cocksucker," and worse — but from that day on, when I did it, we'd both know it was true.

As cocksuckers go, though, he wasn't much. His tongue flicked against my dick in the "let's see whether this tastes nasty" mode. Then he sniffed my crotch for a moment and gave my shaft a big, puppy-dog lap. He might as well have been using a wire hooked up to Hoover Dam. Every nerve ending in my cock had been rubbed raw by weeks of hand jobs that tormented rather than conforted. When his hot, wet tongue flicked against my meat, I knew I would die unless my knob slid deep into Shepherd's farmboy face. I think I surprised the bastard when I didn't put up with his nancy foreplay shit. I didn't have the time. I grabbed a handful of his sweaty hair and rammed everything I had down his throat. He gagged for a minute but his need and throat were big enough to take me without too much trouble. By the time I felt his lips grinding into my stiff red pubes, I felt just fine. I ground my hips against his face and knew I'd found the hole I'd been looking for since I came aboard. He was tight and wet and hot — and, before I finished training him, eager.

His throat started sucking at my pump as the tender tissues of his virgin throat gripped my lizard like a velvet vise. My hips set up their ancient rhythm, sliding my good news into his facehole, then pulling it out about half way so his sandpaper tongue could slide across my hard head. I felt his hands on my butt, both holding me in place and subconsciously exploring his way through undiscovered but inevitable waters. I ground into his friendly fuckhole as one of his hands slipped down to my low-swinging ballbag for a good feel. I slid the bottom of one leg around his shoulder, stroking his sweaty back as my hands grappled with his hair and my dick rammed on. Our scorching metal prison reverberated with my moans as Bob learned how good a man's meat can feel. My lizard down his craw muffled his groans of fresh delight, but his slurping, gurgling noises proved he wasn't about to back out of our deal — as though he could have done with my hands locked around his luscious, cocksucking head. My fuckspeed picked up, slamming his nose harder and faster against my sweat-streaked belly until, without warning, my guts turned inside out and I blasted enough choice sailor spooge down his foxy little throat to satisfy any apprentice sailor-boy cocksucker.

When the first wave hit, I instinctively rammed his face against my belly and held it there as my cock injected my load straight down his throat. I remembered hearing myself scream out shit straight from the most unlikely fuckflicks like *"Oh, Jesus"* and *"suck me harder"* — as if he had a choice. Usually I black out at the critical moment, too busy with enjoying myself to take notes, but every instant of that GQ spooge-shot seared its way into my memory, branding my delight onto my soul. In the decade since, I've replayed it countless times. The image of his fresh face locked around my lizard, the splash of my creamy spunk pulsing up through my cock and blasting down his willing throat, and the feel of his nose against my belly and chin grinding into my tortured ballbag are all as fresh and exciting as they were at our battle stations that fine Navy morning. I ground and gushed and groaned until I thought my dick would rip off at the stub. When I'd slowed to a trickle, I slid my head back into his mouth and ordered him to clean up the leavings with his tongue. The sadistic bastard scraped the broad expanse of my tender head trying to coax more spunk out and, when that didn't work, drilled into my cum-slit after the stragglers. I finally ran dry and eased my joint out of his mouth. I was tempted to fuck with him and pretend there was no way I would touch his dick, but by then the idea of swallowing down his junior-league joint had my 'nades pumping on overtime.

People have compared my dick with an angry cucumber; Shep's was more like a cute carrot, at least in thickness. The whole thing was only six inches long hard; when he went soft, he disappeared to a stub. If you're into size, Bob's not your man. If you like perfect shape, tender juicy foreskins, and a firm lean body dangling off the other end of the dick you mess with, you couldn't find a better candidate for cock of the month. When my lips worked their way around the huge, soft knob of 'skin that hung off the end of Shep's hard, throbbing cock, I felt his body shudder about 9.5 on the Richter scale. My tongue teased the outside of his 'skin for a few seconds and then dived through, sliding between the baby-soft cocksock that protected him from the world and the pulsing, one-eyed lizard that lurked lust-struck below. He'd had a shower before he hit his rack, so his cock was clean enough, but it tasted for all the world like a musky salt lick. We were both sweating so much that the taste of his sweat blended with his manmusk and brewed a broth fit for Olympus. The farther down his trouser-snake my tongue slithered, the louder Shep groaned and moaned and the harder he drilled his dick into my mouth. Too soon for me, he'd gone so far his 'skin folded back across his trigger-ridge like a ragtop in a tornado, leaving his super-tender dickhead open to my mercy. My lips wrapped tight around his crown and slid down on a slick layer of spit — down across his head, over his ridge, across the vein-rich rapids of his 'skin and down his shaft until, his cum-slit snug just inside my throat, I was out of manmeat. I eased up for a few

154

moments and tongued the bejesus out of his head before I started sliding seriously up and down his spit-slicked monorail to cream city. His hands on my head held me down, but I felt *good*.

When I felt his ballbag start slamming into my chin, I knew that if I didn't do something, I'd have a mouth full of his sweet sailor spooge in about three seconds flat. I eased my mouth off his cock and it snapped with a wet thwack up against his bare belly. When he saw I was just taking a breather to give his ballbag a cat-bath, he leaned back against the console and spread his legs wider. Once I was going, it was hard to stop. He had nuts to match his dick — more like a teenager's than a twenty-five year old man's. Each almond-sized gonad hung off a huge, spunk-packed sperm-bag that dwarfed the nut. My tongue practiced my ball-handling technique as I sucked one, then the other into my mouth. I must have been too good, though, because I felt him tighten up again — and I sure as shit wasn't going to have him spunk off while I was screwing with his balls.

Since I was that far down, I spread him a bit more and snaked my tongue back toward his butt. I'm not usually into rimming, but Bob's shower and the salty taste of his sweat convinced me he should be a special case. To really get at him, I turned him around and draped his chest across the console. When I got my first close-up look at his butt, I knew I'd found my dream man for the deployment. It was one of those tight, hard asses that pops straight out from the waist with real handfuls of muscle and zero fat. As my fingers parted the muscle and my nose and tongue slid between them, I found a hard, swampy paradise. He was as clean as I'd expected, and completely hairless, sopping with enough sweat to make Johnstown worry. I think he expected me to fuck him on the spot and wasn't sure what to do about it, but when he realized I had my tongue up his butt, he went wild, grinding his soggy pink pucker against my lips. My tongue darted here and there, trying to dance around his butthole, but he'd had foreplay and was ready for a tongue-fuck. Shep was so innocent-looking, I knew he'd never even dreamed of being rimmed out before ; but once the idea took hold, he wasn't about to turn loose of it. When he worked the flesh of his fuckhole onto my tongue, those tender folds were ready to spindle and muti-late. His butt grabbed my tongue and lured it into him as far as the massive muscles of his butt would allow. He rubbed against my face, purring like a kitten on cream and getting more wound up by the second.

His butt was nice, but I didn't want him getting *too* happy until he was inside my mouth. I whirled his ass around and popped his cock back into my mouth. My fuckfingers slid back and into his fuckhole to keep it occupied while I cranked my sucker into overdrive. The Navy had taught young Shep a lot of words, and he used most of them as he was sliding in and out of my facehole. He got progressively louder and more profane until I felt his butt clench tight around my hands, heard him scream out in agony, and felt the most glorious taste in the cosmos flood my mouth. His cock couldn't quite reach far enough back to fire down my throat, so everything he blasted off the back of my throat and flooded back down to splash across my tastebuds until I was drowning in white, creamy, manly glory. I held him inside me, building the pressure of his spunk until my cheeks bulged before I started to swallow. I could only imagine the way his cock had to feel, trapped in a pressurized mouthful of his own juicy jetting jism. While he was transforming me from a cocksucker into a awallower, my hands eagerly tore as his butt. I had plans for that hole, too, and didn't want him to forget the itch that lived alone, lurking deep inside it.

After what seemed like gallons but can only have been six inches' worth, he finally ran dry. I messed with him for awhile, cleaning him off, tenderly tormenting him with my tongue, and generally getting in a few last good licks; but we both knew he'd shot his wad.

I pried my face off his dick and thanked him kindly. Just as I knew the greedy bastard would do, he suggested we try it again. I wasn't having any. Would he like to fuck me up the butt? His green eyes almost popped out and he did everything but drool. I only had one catch. Once he'd done me, I was going to ream his butt until he puked spooge for a week. Fear crinkled the corner of his eyes, but lust won out and forced his head into a resigned, solemn, nod. I lay down on the deck and let him slide between my legs. We both still had our dungarees around our ankles and, somehow, I liked it that way. Fucking in our uniforms was even more wicked and delightful. When I'd nestled my boondockers against his but, I was tempted to reach up with my lips to meet his. I knew not to take him too fast however strong my craving. It was enough to lie there with him above me and feel his cute little cock slide into me. I'm really a cocksucker at heart and have found that most dicks are more than my butt can accommodate comfortably. Shep's entire body seemed made to complement mine. I could feel him just fine, but he felt snug, not as though he were ripping my insides out.

When he started sliding in and out, slamming his hips into my ass harder with every stroke, I kept my eyes locked onto his as he saw the dawning of wisdom. In that first minute or two up my butt, Shepherd discovered what he'd been missing all his life. My hands slid over his sweat-slicked body, tearing at his tits, gliding along his flanks, and holding tight to his back as he fucked into me. His hips rose and fell in counterpoint to my yearning, in harmony with his growing croons of sublime sensual delight. At last I couldn't resist any longer and reached my face up toward his, locking my lips around his ear lobe. I sucked like a fiend at his ear while my hot, lust-racked breath boiled into his consciousness. He lost all control over his body and fucked into my butt like the savage he was destined to become, heedless of my comfort or delight, driven only by his instinctive animal needs. For the first time in my life, I'd found a dick that felt *good* up my butt. I'd worried about friction, but he harder he pounded, the better I felt. In the blissful violence of that rut, I found peace at last — dangling like a slut off the end of his cock. He filled my need, scratched my secret itch, and warmed my butt with a glow that grew hotter with every stroke. Too soon for either of us, I felt his breath turn to a snarl as his hips lost their cadence. Spasm after spasm rocked my buddy's lust-racked body until one final, feral, almost endless cry rent the suffocating air of our compartment as Bob Shepherd scored the first buttfuck of his life. From some secret cache of studly yearning, he summoned another massive load of cock-cream to splatter up deep into my guts. I milked his manmeat udderly dry and kept on squeezing his bone as he kept dogging my hole, slamming away in me on autopilot.

My feet held his ass down until I remembered that I had a hole to fill myself. When he slid out and splashed his lean body down into the pool of sweat I had become, I held him in my arms for a few moments while he caught his breath. I wiped a sodden shock of hair off his brow and asked him how it felt to be a cocksucker. He smiled and asked me how it felt to be a walking buttfuck. That, of course, was my signal to move in to claim my prize. I didn't rush up his ass. My meat takes some getting used to, so I went back with the fingers, pulling and pushing and stretching his virgin shithole until it was the finest seapussy in the Gulf. It was mine. By the time I'd made a man out of Shep, GQ was over and it was time for quarters. We both stood watch all day wearing each other's sweat and dried jism — and loving every second of it. The CO kept having GQ's because he was pissed that the Navy couldn't find some way to sail into Tehran and kick ass. Shep and I were the only two aboard who didn't mind if we stayed at GQ thirty-six hours a day. We knew that kicking ass was a waste of time — not to mention ass.

BOOKS FROM LEYLAND PUBLICATIONS/G.S. PRESS

☐ **MEATMEN Anthology of Gay Male Comics.** Volumes 1, 2, 3, 4, 5, 6, 7, 8, 9, 10, 11, 12, 13. Tom of Finland, Stephen, etc. Large-sized books. $16.95 each, postpaid. Circle vols. wanted.

☐ **UNDER THE COVERS/BETWEEN THE SHEETS.** Comics by Kurt Erichsen and Bruce Billings in one large volume. $11.95.

☐ **MOVIE STAR CONFIDENTIAL** Comics by Mike/**SUPER ADVENTURES OF HARRY CHESS** Comics by A. Jay. Large-sized collection of sexcomics by two famous artists. $11.95.

☐ **OH BOY!** Sex Comics by a new wave artist, Brad Parker. $11.95.

☐ **TRASH/TRUCKER/SEXSTOP/HEADSTOPS/HOTTRICKS: True Revelations & Strange Happenings from** *18 Wheeler,* Vols. 1–5. Ed. by John Dagion. Hot true sex stories. $11.95 each. Circle titles wanted.

☐ **CRYSTAL BOYS** by Pai Hsien-Yung. The first Chinese novel on gay themes — a moving story of adolescent boys driven to hustling. $13.95.

☐ **ENLISTED MEAT: True Homosexual Military Stories.** Read what marines, soldiers, sailors do to each other. $14.95.

☐ **SEX BEHIND BARS** by Robert N. Boyd. True stories of male-male sex in prison. $16.95.

☐ **CUM / JUICE / WADS / CREAM.** Best-selling **True Homosexual Experiences from** *S.T.H.* Edited by Boyd McDonald (circle the ones wanted). $13.00 each.

☐ **HOT ACTS / ORGASMS / HOT STUDS / SINGLEHANDED: Homosexual Encounters from** *First Hand* Vols. 1–4. $11.95 each.

☐ **HARD / MANPLAY / YOUNG NUMBERS / HUMONGOUS / 10½ INCHES / BOYS! BOYS! BOYS! / STUDFLESH / BOYS WILL BE BOYS / EIGHTEEN AND OVER: True Gay Encounters** Vols. 2–10. Hot male-male sex stories. $12.95 each. Circle books wanted.

☐ **CUT/UNCUT: True Gay Experiences of Foreskin & Circumcision.** Illustrated. $11.00.

☐ **SURFER SEX / AUSSIE BOYS / AUSSIE HOT.** Gay Encounters from Australia by Rusty Winter. $29.95 for all three books.

☐ **STAND BY YOUR MAN** & other stories by Jack Fritscher. Radical sex, lyrical love. $11.00. (Also by same author: **CORPORAL IN CHARGE OF TAKING CARE OF CAPTAIN O'MALLEY.** $11.00.)

☐ **THE DELIGHT OF HEARTS.** Stories of boy prostitutes and others in ancient Araby by Ahmad al-Tifashi. $12.00.

☐ **GAY ROOTS: TWENTY YEARS OF GAY SUNSHINE: An Anthology of Gay History, Sex, Politics, and Culture.** Large 700-page collection of work by 100 + writers, artists: in-depth articles, fiction, essays, poetry by the best writers of the past two decades. A landmark book. Illustrated. $25.95.

TO ORDER: Check books wanted (or list them on a separate sheet) and send check/money order to Leyland Publications, P.O. Box 410690, San Francisco, CA 94141. **Postage included in prices quoted.** Calif. residents add 7% sales tax. Mailed in unmarked book envelopes. Add $1 for complete catalogue.

AIDS RISK REDUCTION GUIDELINES
FOR HEALTHIER SEX

As given by Bay Area Physicians for Human Rights
and reprinted from *In the Heat of Passion: How to Have Hotter, Safer Sex.*

NO RISK. *Most of these activities involve only skin-to-skin contact, thereby avoiding exposure to blood, semen, and vaginal secretions. This assumes there are no breaks in the skin.* **1) Social kissing** (dry). **2) Body massage, hugging. 3) Body to body rubbing** (frottage). **4) Light S&M** (without bruising or bleeding). **5) Using one's own sex toys. 6) Mutual masturbation** (male or external female). Care should be taken to avoid exposing the partners to ejaculate or vaginal secretions. Seminal, vaginal and salivary fluids should not be used as lubricants.

LOW RISK. *In these activities small amounts of certain body fluids might be exchanged, or the protective barrier might break causing some risk.* **1) Anal or vaginal intercourse with condom.** Risk is incurred if the condom breaks or if semen spills into the rectum or vagina. The risk is further reduced if one withdraws before climax. **2) Fellatio interruptus** (sucking, stopping before climax). Pre-ejaculate fluid may contain HIV. Saliva may contain HIV in low concentration. The insertive partner should warn the receptive partner before climax to prevent exposure to a large volume of semen. If mouth or genital sores are present, risk is increased. Likewise, action which causes mouth or genital injury will increase risk. **3) Fellatio with condom** (sucking with condom). Risk is low unless breakage occurs. **4) Mouth-to-mouth kissing** (French kissing, wet kissing). HIV is present in saliva in such low concentration that salivary exchange is unlikely to transmit the virus. Risk is increased if sores in the mouth or bleeding gums are present. **5) Oral-vaginal or oral-anal contact with protective barrier.** e.g. a latex dam, obtainable through a dental supply house. Do not reuse latex barrier. **6) Manual anal contact with glove** (fisting with glove). If the glove does not break, virus transmission should not occur. However, significant trauma can still be inflicted on the rectal tissues leading to other medical problems. **7) Manual vaginal contact with glove** (internal). See above.

MODERATE RISK. *These activities involve tissue trauma and/or exchange of body fluids which may transmit HIV or other sexually transmitted disease.* **1) Fellatio** (sucking to climax). Semen may contain high concentrations of HIV and if absorbed through open sores in the mouth or digestive tract could pose risk. **2) Oral-anal contact** (rimming). HIV may be contained in blood-contaminated feces or in the anal rectal lining. This practice also poses high risk of transmission of parasites and other gastrointestinal infections. **3) Cunnilingus** (oral-vaginal contact). Vàginal secretions and menstrual blood have been shown to harbor HIV, thereby causing risk to the oral partner if open lesions are present in the mouth or digestive tract. **4) Manual rectal contact** (fisting). Studies have indicated a direct association between fisting and HIV infection for both partners. This association may be due to concurrent use of recreational drugs, bleeding, pre-fisting semen exposure, or anal intercourse with ejaculation. **5) Sharing sex toys. 6) Ingestion of urine.** HIV has not been shown to be transmitted via urine; however, other immunosuppressive agents or infections may be transmitted in this manner.

HIGH RISK. *These activities have been shown to transmit HIV.* **1) Receptive anal intercourse without condom.** All studies imply that this activity carries the highest risk of transmitting HIV. **2) Insertive anal intercourse without condom.** Studies suggest that men who participate only in this activity are at less risk of being infected than their partners who are rectally receptive; however the risk is still significant. It carries high risk of infection by other sexually transmitted diseases. **3) Vaginal intercourse without condom.**

Sex is an important part of our lives. We owe it to ourselves and to our partners to keep it as healthy (low risk) as we can.